CERAMICS

✻ PROFILES of POTTERS and ARTISANS ✻

VANESSA VILLARREAL, KAITLYN BRENNAN

ENCYCLOPEDIA OF INSPIRATION

UPPERCASE

**CERAMICS
VOLUME "C"**

POLLY FERN, NAOMI CLEMENT

**encyclopediaofinspiration.com
uppercasemagazine.com**

UPPERCASE PUBLISHING INC

201B – 908, 17th Avenue SW
Calgary, Alberta, Canada T2T 0A3

©2020 UPPERCASE publishing inc

This book may not be reproduced in any manner without written permission. You are welcome to share photos of this book in your life on Instagram: #encyclopediaofinspiration #uppercaseceramics @uppercasemag

Art and photography copyright belongs to the artists.

PRINTED IN CANADA BY THE PROLIFIC GROUP

WRITTEN BY
CAROLE EPP
JULIA KRUEGER

DESIGN
JANINE VANGOOL

COPYEDITING
CORREY BALDWIN

SANDRA APPERLOO, MARINE BOSSU

PIGEON TOE CERAMICS

CONTENTS

INTRODUCTION 10

NARRATIVE
POLLY FERN 22
VANESSA VILLARREAL 32
JULIE WHITMORE 40
MEL ROBSON 46
AARON CALDWELL 54
JAPNEET KAUR 64
MARINE BOSSU 74
LYNNE HOBAICA
& RICKIE BARNETT 84

NATURE
MORGAN DOANE 96
BRIDGET FAIRBANK 104
PATRICIA GRIFFIN 114
VICKI GRIMA 120
JULIE MOON 128
SARAH PIKE 136
SARAH RAYNER 144

LIFE/WORK BALANCE
HEATHER DAHL 156
NAOMI CLEMENT 164
ROBIN DUPONT 174
KATE FISHER 184
DEBRA KUZYK
& RAY MACKIE 190
SHED POTTERY 198
JUSTIN ROTHSHANK 206
HADIYA WILLIAMS 214

LESS IS MORE

KALIKA BOWLBY	*224*
JACKIE FRIOUD	*232*
NORIKO MASUDA	*240*
NATALIE J WOOD	*248*
INGRID WENS	*254*
NATHAN WILLEVER	*262*
PIGEON TOE CERAMICS	*270*

MORE IS MORE

ZUZKA VACLAVIK	*282*
ASHLEY KIM	*290*
LYDIA JOHNSON	*298*
MEGAN BOGONOVICH	*308*
SHANNON BUTLER	*316*
PATTIE CHALMERS	*324*
TANYA EVERARD	*334*
ALISON HUNTER	*342*
JANICE JAKIELSKI	*350*
KYLE JOHNS	*360*

JOY

SANDRA APPERLOO	*370*
INGELA ARRHENIUS	*376*
KAITLYN BRENNAN	*384*
DEBORAH FISHER	*392*
ADRIENNE ELIADES	*400*
RICHARD NICKEL	*408*

ACKNOWLEDGEMENTS	*414*
AUTHOR BIOS	*416*

MEL ROBSON

CAROLE EPP & JULIA KRUEGER

CERAMICS

Ceramics are found everywhere. The art form has a rich and extensive history in cultures around the world, and yet there are other, more modern reasons why artists remain drawn to it today—to the material, as well as to ceramics as a profession and form of creative expression. Perhaps it is the material's malleability and unlimited potential. Or perhaps it is how, no matter the approach, ceramics—and the clay they are made from—have the power to reach back and echo the voices of the past, all the while presenting evocative references to the here and now.

In the pages of this book, you will find artists and artwork to inspire you. Some may surprise you, others will feel as comfortable as a well-worn sweater or an old friend. That is the power of handmade objects. They may be humble in their function or making, yet they affect us greatly through their infiltration into our daily and personal lives.

There are 46 profiles in this book, and each artist has their own unique approach to working in clay, and has taken their own path toward a successful artistic career—one that has been as individual as their own creative vision. Many of the artists have other creative pursuits and skill sets, yet clay is their focal point. It is what connects them all, regardless of where they live, what culture or community they come from, what stage of life they are in, or what they make, be it functional objects for domestic day-to-day use or sculptures destined for display in a gallery.

Countless decisions go into a project such as this book. Narrowing down the selection of artists was an undertaking that involved months of curation and selection from a call for entries. The publication could

RICKIE BARNETT

have been completed a hundred times over, with a new group of equally incredible artists each time. There is no easy method for narrowing down selections, and in the end, we aimed to thoughtfully consider various stages of career, stylistic approaches, technical innovation and diversity.

Each artist profiled in this Encyclopedia of Inspiration has a story to tell. From the beginning of this project, it was clear that there would be a focus on narrative. However, we also noticed a number of other unifying themes, or lenses with which to examine the work, and we ended up organizing the book into six sections, which we see as a reflection of themes within the field of ceramics today: Narrative, Nature, Life/Work Balance, Less is More, More is More and Joy.

NARRATIVE

The first section presents a broad range of approaches to subject matter, from the personal to the universal. There are stories of wonder, as well as of the struggles of the human condition, in its multitude of perspectives, all told through ceramics. You'll be taken from the outback of Australia, where Mel Robson's work uses landscape and mapping as a metaphor for the passage of time and the human experience, to North Carolina, where Lynne Hobaica and Rickie Barnett delve deeply and vulnerably into their upbringings through their functional and sculptural work. Polly Fern, Marine Bossu, Julie Whitmore and Vanessa Villarreal create magical, joyous worlds from their studios in the UK, France, the USA and Canada. Each artist has their own underpinnings of moral tales, life experiences and personal iconography that shape their artwork. The imagery they produce is so rich it seems to be pulled from lavish paintings, watercolour palettes or vivid illustration, yet through the ceramic material, it becomes frozen in time as a permanent record of precise yet universal moments.

JAPNEET KAUR

The artists Japneet Kaur and Aaron Caldwell offer up so much truth and bravery in the presentation of their personal journeys, both creating space for dialogue and for the representation of BIPOC stories—those of Black, Indigenous and people of colour—within the medium and their communities. Japneet weaves her narrative of immigration to Canada through her characters and recurring symbolism. Both emotionally and, through complex metaphor, intellectually, she delves into intimate narratives about defining home and the struggle of refugees. Aaron Caldwell creates "faux pots" that reference art traditions from Africa to America and that become contemporary self-portraits of his life as a young, Black, queer artist and educator.

NATURE

In one way or another, the environment, plants and animals play an important role in the work and creative lives of the artists included in the Nature section. For Patricia Griffin of Cambria, California, and Vicki Grima of Sydney, Australia, the ocean serves as a restorative and inspirational presence. In addition, the undulating organic forms of Vicki's pinched vessels and brooches echo the landscape and the ocean-worn shells and rocks of her environment. As with Patricia's woodcut-like surfaces, which team with tactile, nature-filled narrative potential, texture is also a key consideration in the work of Sarah Pike. Both ceramists use texture adeptly, but their processes differ, as Patricia carves her designs into leather-hard clay while Sarah stamps into wet slabs with her custom-made stamps, many of which relate to the natural world around her in Fernie, British Columbia.

The environment has also played an important role in the relational work of Bridget Fairbank, whose

BRIDGET FAIRBANK

JULIE MOON

installations and happenings are inspired by her time living in Florida and working as a fire spotter in Northern Alberta. Nature's bounty in the form of plants and food serves as a uniting metaphor within her work, and reminds us that we are a part of nature. Sarah Rayner's fecund porcelain sculptures speak to the wondrous power of nature and are inspired by the bushland of Australia, where she lives, works and collects. Her acute sense of detail and considered arrangement of multiple pod forms and collections requires attentive, close observation, much like the enchanted looking that takes place in a natural history museum.

For Morgan Doane and Julie Moon, it is not so much the outdoor environment around them but cultural mediations on nature and the domestic that serve as a foundation for their plant-inspired practices. For Morgan, a self-professed house plant enthusiast, taking up ceramics was a way for her to provide her beloved plants with handmade homes, designed with both aesthetics and the plant in mind. Julie's fictive florals burst with life as they combine a 1960s and '70s aesthetic with her appreciation for graphic and textile design, pointing to just how influential nature is in design. Whether it be a walk along the beach or in an otherworldly wilderness filled with Pop Art and porcelain pods, nature in all its variety nourishes these artists' work.

LIFE/WORK BALANCE

While some artists are fuelled by the isolation of a quiet studio, others find their passion in collaborative endeavours with fellow artists, industries and creatives. The balance between work and life is an unending quest for most artists, one that adapts and changes with the seasons of our lives. The artists in the Life/Work Balance section share with us a glimpse into those attempts at balance, the successes and failures, and how collaborations that inspire and support creative processes are formed.

We uncover stories of the endless possibilities of sustainable studio practice, from Kate Fisher, whose attempts to find balance as a mother and artist led her to create a resource for other creative mothers, to Heather Dahl, who has balanced motherhood, creative work and business management, all while living and working in Vancouver, one of the world's most expensive cities. Justin Rothshank has found balance through stewardship of the land on which he lives, and through creative pursuits that are both politically motivated and charity driven. Also closely tied to the land is Robin Dupont, who has created a studio and home life in the Slocan Valley in the mountains of British Columbia, where he can focus on teaching and intensive research into firing techniques. From Naomi Clement who is for the first time hanging up her travelling shoes to set up a home studio, to Johann Munro carrying on a family tradition, to Hadiya Williams who is creating a lifestyle brand across multiple materials, to Deb Kuzyk who has been a staple in her community for decades and is newly adapting to provide opportunities for other artists; we trace lives in clay and map pathways to long-term sustainability.

LESS IS MORE

Architect Mies van der Rohe is credited with the phrase "less is more" to refer to his modern architectural style, and the phrase has since become associated with a minimalist aesthetic, in which things are pared down to their essentials. In reaction to minimalism, another architect, Robert Venturi, coined the postmodern maxim "less is a bore," but as we discovered with the ceramists in this section, while their aesthetic might be minimal, their work and practices are far from boring!

INTRODUCTION   15

Jackie Frioud and Nathan Willever both maintain a balance between control and chaos within their work. Jackie embraces all the unknowns that come with atmospherically firing her work in a salt kiln, and Nathan, along with wood firing some of his wares, uses "wild" materials that he gathers and mines himself. Natalie Wood's exacting forms and beautiful surfaces can stand on their own, but she also actively engages with a sense of the unknown by inviting other artists to add illustrations to her pots. Just as poets can say so much in so few words, Kalika Bowlby visually communicates the understated beauty of the natural world through her skillfully designed vessels and cool colour palette. When designing her functional pottery, Ingrid Wens pares down to the essentials. Through her innovative use of the Rijksmuseum's vast digital archive, she negotiates the fine line of how little visual and tactile information one needs in order to access personal and cultural memories.

Minimalism is also often associated with industrial production, and two makers within this group, Noriko Masuda and Lisa Jones, create work that is closely associated both physically and aesthetically with industry. While the visibly handmade is often celebrated in ceramics, and craft in general, Noriko's exacting processes (many of which relate to ceramics' industrial history) and her drive for perfection showcase her "invisible hand." Lisa's company, Pigeon Toe Ceramics (a sister-led, female-powered ceramic design and manufacturing studio), produces minimal ceramic housewares such as modern ceramic pendant lamps. Her ceramics speak to William Morris' sage advice to have nothing in your house that is not useful or beautiful. The artists in this section demonstrate that when it comes to ceramics, less is definitely more!

MORE IS MORE

In contrast to the previous section, the makers featured in this section push things to the max. They reference, remix, elaborate, layer and reinterpret. Their visual feasts push pattern and decoration to new heights, while also appealing to a variety of senses. Zuzka Vaclavik, Tanya Everard, Shannon Butler and Lydia Johnson all explore surface decoration and the myriad of ways it can be approached. Although Zuzka is fairly new to clay, she brings an attention to surface that is informed by her background in painting. Tanya uses 19th-century pattern books as inspiration for her pattern designs, which she then expertly applies to her forms, enhancing their vessel-like qualities. Shannon's aesthetic can best be described as playful, eclectic, bright, layered and bohemian-inspired, and her functional pieces are not only a joy to look at but are fun to feel as well. Lydia covers the interiors and exteriors of her functional ceramic wares with bright, graphic all-over pattern work, which she prints onto both sides of a slab of clay before fashioning it into a form.

Ashley Kim plays with stereotypical functional forms by reinterpreting them and then covering the new yet familiar forms with bold colours and all-over pattern work. There is a sense of the infinite in Kyle Johns' work, as, like the work of the Cubists, every angle, view and exterior surface appears to be sectioned over and over again.

Ceramic sculpture is also explored in this section with the work of Pattie Chalmers and Megan Bogonovich. Both ceramists incorporate the concept of multiplicity within their work. Megan combines multiple parts into a larger whole to create sculptures with an "alien floral vibe," and Pattie, in addition to creating her functional work, which she covers in intricate patterns, recently created a ceramic installation, with 365 separately sculpted objects.

ALISON HUNTER

More is More also examines how artists are pushing the field of ceramics through their processes and subject matter. Alison Hunter repairs, remixes and rejuvenates ceramic shards that are otherwise seen as broken, useless and incomplete, turning them into mixed-media works that complicate time and history. Janice Jakielski pushes the material itself to do more. With her current body of work, she has adapted the industrial process of tape casting in order to create impossibly thin porcelain sculptures that also speak to the layered history of porcelain. Although More is More covers a wide range of processes, approaches and material, what unites all these artists is a sense of pushing boundaries, and the complexities that this produces: there's always more to do, more space to cover and more pieces to put together.

JOY

Some artists rely on humour and playfulness to greet their audiences. Bright colours and forms aside, there is much more to these works than one might think. Humour and joy radiate through the objects these artists create, inspiring new levels of connecting with each other. In this section you will find the work of Richard Nickel, who straddles comedy and tragedy in his signature style in order to stop his audience in their tracks and have them reconsider their relationships, both natural or interpersonal. He has created a unique, bold aesthetic that moves playfully and effortlessly between ceramics, 2D murals, animations and zine culture.

Adrienne Eliades' flawless yet quirky designs create a sense of joyfulness through their use, as she makes objects with a direct correlation to the food they will serve. Deborah Fisher, on the other hand, is a maker for other makers. Her animated ceramic characters and critters are designed to enliven the studios

DEBORAH FISHER

of other creatives. Both Kaitlyn Brennan and Sandra Apperloo use pattern and image extensively—Kaitlyn creating visually layered and sometimes hilariously subtle and subversive work, and Sandra using her years of curating a design blog to inform her visual language and practice. Joy and childhood nostalgia are tightly linked in the work of Ingela Arrhenius, who effortlessly transfers her acclaimed illustrations of vintage life onto charming vintage ceramic objects.

After reading through the profiles and taking in the delicious images of each and every artist, we hope that you will come away with a sense of just how all-encompassing the field of ceramics is, as it includes everything from sculpture to housewares, to jewellery, installations, illustration and community engagement. The materials and processes associated with ceramics are endless as well, and within these pages you will find information on atmospheric firings, casting and specific clay bodies. You may even be surprised by a few examples, and thus encouraged to reevaluate your own definition of ceramics.

Through the course of this project, we, too, found ourselves reevaluating how we defined ceramics, and in the process we learned so much from the participating artists. We are thrilled with the honesty and vulnerability with which each artist approached their discussions with us. It is an honour to help tell their stories here. ✤

AARON CALDWELL

NARRATIVE

WRITTEN BY CAROLE EPP

MODERN VICTORIAN

POLLY FERN

Inspired by the historical pottery forms and styling of Victorian transferware, Polly Fern creates a modern twist on tradition with her unique illustrated ceramics. Creating work out of her garden studio in the United Kingdom, the illustrator and ceramicist has built a name for herself exhibiting her work internationally, including at the MET Museum of Art in New York and with design company Tonkachi in Japan.

Polly studied illustration at university, with ceramics only becoming a part of her practice after she signed up for an evening class. She discovered that her love of illustration paired beautifully with her desire to work more physically with material in her hands. Ceramics gave Polly a better way to depict her imagery and stories. Plates, tiles and vessels became the perfect framing devices for her illustrations, and her love of antique British ceramics provided more content and aesthetic direction within which to develop her work.

LOVE OF THE LAND

For her illustrations, Polly is inspired by different places she has visited, childhood stories, elaborate and well-tended gardens, and her Whippet dog and pet canaries. Polly's work depicts the specific charm of the English countryside, but the narrative of labour and love of the land that she portrays has universal appeal. "Plants and gardening have always been a presence in my work," she says. "The tools people use, the way something is grown and the structure and colours that come from the craft of gardening are forever present in my work."

"I think my work is there to make people feel warm and nostalgic. I imagine that my work attracts people who like to create a home, and who might have a particular interest in people's stories and history."

CERAMIC HISTORY AS INSPIRATION

Polly's pets show up in the lines of the small sculpted ornaments she makes. This work is informed by her love of Staffordshire figurines: "I find Staffordshire figurines particularly charming, how the characters are all taken from moulds and duplicated hundreds of times, but are all hand-painted. I enjoy the variation within the same characters and how they have strange expressions upon their faces, or how a design has been painted by someone so many times that the detail comes to look not quite right, somewhat unusual and comical. This is something that I try to maintain within my work. I like to paint characters or animals from memory rather than from a photograph, as the characters tend to become their own species and then feature as ongoing motifs throughout all my work."

UPBRINGING IN CRAFT AND ANTIQUING

Polly constantly has her eye out for new inspiration: she takes trips to local antique dealers, where she can delve into her love of Victorian transferware; she looks to historic buildings for their intricate sculpted facades; and she studies vintage ornate furniture and highly decorated spaces. The influence of textiles, wallpaper patterns and domestic life in particular can be found in her work. Much of Polly's love of history stems from her father, a cabinet maker, and his passion for such things. When Polly was a child, her father would bring her along on his adventures, which fuelled her lifestyle of antiquing, her involvement in craft education and her attention to detail.

"My ceramics are very reflective of my personality and often depict or are inspired by my everyday life. In the stories and scenes, I often feature our family's pet Whippets and my beloved canary companions."

FROM PAPER TO CLAY

Polly starts by drawing in her sketchbooks, transforming her plethora of visual inspiration into black line drawings. Before taking the imagery to the clay surface, Polly cuts out paper templates, using them to work out the challenges of integrating proportion, shape and surface to form.

"Once I have created the shape, I will make a little ceramic test tile, which I like to call Miniature Framed Paintings," she says. "I have a big box full of them, which are like treasure to me, as it's where all of my illustrative ideas begin for the designs upon my ceramics pieces."

Polly's ceramic forms are hand-built from slabs of white earthenware clay. This clay body contains no grit, thus the surfaces remain smooth to the touch and do not interfere with Polly's illustration techniques. The clay also allows her to obtain brighter colours when combining a tin glaze with a lower temperature firing.

Polly currently creates two lines of work: her Paper Cut Garden Stories collection and her Romantic Tin Glazed collection. For the first collection, Polly developed a collage-style technique of cutting out intricate paper stencils and combining them with pigmented slips. With the second collection she uses a loose painting style, allowing each work to become a unique piece of art. Polly restricts her colour palette to three or four colours, which also helps keep the illustrations from becoming too busy or visually overwhelming. Using a slip trailer on the pots, Polly creates decorative relief borders that reference Victorian transferware. The simple white tin glaze that she uses overtop highlights these tactile decorative elements both subtly and beautifully. ❋

"My favourite clay body will always be a smooth white earthenware. I love the elasticity of the clay, but it can be a challenge to work with when hand-building. Tin glaze will always be my favourite, and my most-used piece of equipment is my surgical scalpel blade!"

"I run a business freelancing in illustration, and doing exhibitions and selling my ceramic artworks. Upon graduating I went straight into freelancing in illustration, but I also joined the ceramic studio. This was key for me to have my eggs in different creative baskets, and initially it helped me to get income streams from both areas. I would have struggled freelancing in illustration alone. I now see illustration and ceramics as one in my creative business and life."

pollyfern.com
@pollyfern

GARDEN STUDIO

I work alone and create every single ceramic piece that comes out of my studio. I moved into my first home in 2019, and after many years of sharing a studio, decided to build my own in the garden. It's a wooden framed building with black painted cladding on the outside. It's surrounded by my plants in my garden, which make me feel calm and happy whilst working.

I have a studio space inside the house where I create my "clean" illustration work. Sometimes I may spend a solid week in there painting or doing admin work and packaging my online shop orders. Another week I may be in the ceramic studio making. It really varies week to week, which I love, as it means you never get bored!

LOVE POEMS IN PORCELAIN

VANESSA VILLARREAL

Vanessa Villarreal was born and raised in the Sacramento Valley of California and currently lives in Gatineau, Quebec, with her husband and two sons. "We moved here in 2016 after living some years in Tucson, Arizona, where I had a small pottery studio and my husband was in graduate school," Vanessa says. "I am still adjusting to life in Canada and particularly living in a Francophone society, but I am working on my French and loving the slower pace of life that Canada brings us. My husband is from Quebec, and we decided to move here because I felt the mother/artist balance would be easier here than in America." In Canada she finds more opportunities and supports, such as healthcare and subsidized daycare.

Vanessa took a three-year break from ceramics when she had her children. "I couldn't do it all—teaching, having a business, wrangling babies and moving three times—without losing myself," she recalls. "So I chose motherhood first. When I got back into a studio when we arrived in Montreal, I worked for over a year getting to know the clay and ceramic community in Canada. A new direction of my work started to happen and I jumped back into selling and teaching."

Vanessa describes her ceramics as "small love poems in cup or dish form." Not simply functional and sculptural objects, they are haikus praising the beauty of nature, sonnets of the world of mysticism, miniature tableaus that speak quietly yet evocatively of themes of love, the home and dreams for the future. Each piece is filled with her own iconography, including chairs, ladders and flowers. "The symbols of moths, moons and snakes, combined with a feminine hand, is my poem about emotions and intuition. It is

"I think the nature of play and investigation keeps artists making work, and for me this is especially true. I am never bored and I feel I am problem-solving almost every minute of my day. Teaching also helps keep things in perspective, as it is a thrill to see people get hooked on clay!"

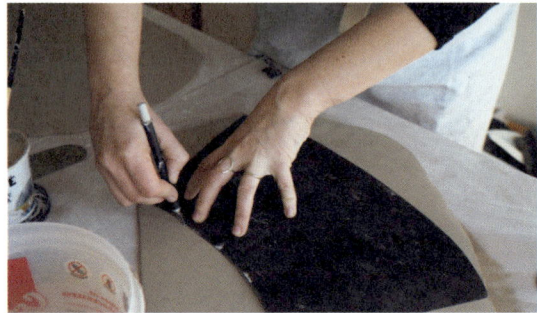

my way of communicating and saying to others: I feel you, my hand is reaching to the stars and flowers, too. My work touches on a yearning and curiosity about spiritualism, intuition and feminism."

She was introduced to ceramics at an early age by her grandmother, who was a jeweller and ceramicist. "She was earthy, eccentric and made a lot of pottery in the 1970s and 1980s," Vanessa says. "My home was filled with creative sculptures and dishes from my grandmother. She was a unique influence in my life. She loved collecting bones and shells and rocks, and was inspired by a modern Japanese aesthetic. Nothing she ever made was cute or exactly pretty in the way one might assume a grandmother would create. Her decorative patterns were often made from fish bones or seedpods, and many of her glazes were dark. I find I am similar to her in my love of decoration on surfaces, but our work is totally opposite in colour and texture. I inherited many of her tools and bones, and her handmade stamps that I use daily on my ceramics. So her spirit is still alive and working with me in my studio now."

Nowadays Vanessa is well recognized for her unique ceramics, but she did not always feel confident about the aesthetic of her work or the direction it was taking. "My work is overtly feminine," she says. "It has taken years to just own that idea and embrace decorating my ceramics this way. For years I thought what I was making was too cute or immature, and this was making me feel stuck in my work. With practice I now listen to a voice in me that is full of flowers, glittery gold, clouds and rainbows, and I am feeling pretty strong about what I make now."

"Creating work brings me such joy. I wake up every morning thrilled to get to work."

VANESSA VILLARREAL

STUDIO PROCESS

Vanessa tends not to sketch, but rather starts with paper and scissors, collaging the different elements together, figuring out the scale for the final clay piece. Her workspace tabletop is filled with miniature paper cutouts—painted references for their clay counterparts. "I will cut moths or butterflies and arrange them with moons and chairs or clouds, and see if a story I like emerges," she explains. "Unexpected things emerge and I feel more playful with the work. Then I trace the cutouts and templates I like best onto thick watercolour paper or tar paper and use these to guide me when I cut them on a clay slab." Vanessa has always been drawn to hand-building her objects, as she can carve out a studio space just about anywhere, including at the kitchen table as the blur and frenzy of life with two young children surrounds her.

PORCELAIN AND MUTED COLOURS

The porcelain clay Vanessa uses is a perfect fit for her cups, bowls and wall pieces. The crisp whiteness of the material echoes paper-cut art and collage. There is a delicacy to her imagery that is reinforced in the fragility of porcelain. Her narrative collages are moments and ideas, frozen in time, like ghosts in white porcelain, highlighted through a calculated use of a minimal colour palette to bring them to life.

ONE-OF-A-KIND WORKS

Vanessa does not make production or large-scale work, partially because of her studio and kiln restrictions, but also because she feels that her current method of working inspires playfulness and allows for experimentation. She tends to sell directly to her customers through markets or online, and finds that the direct interaction and feedback she receives helps inspire her to return to the studio every day. In 2019 she collaborated with Anthropologie on a body of work for their stores, but otherwise has not yet had the desire to make a tableware or production line, preferring to focus her energy on creating one-of-a-kind objects, and the joy that it brings. For Vanessa, each piece is a new story to tell, a new poem to present. "As a very shy and quiet woman, I have difficulty expressing myself verbally," she says. "Most days I would rather not talk at all, so for me, making this work is about finding a strong voice and sharing ideas with others." ✳

villarrealceramics.com
@villarrealceramics

BUSINESS

Vanessa sells her ceramics online, at select retail spaces and at local markets. She also teaches hand-building in community ceramic studios. "For many years I had part-time jobs in retail, too, as it relieved the pressure of having to be more aggressive in selling work," she says. "Now I balance teaching one to two classes a week, being a mom and having a business."

She has taken her time growing the business. "I am a cautious person and a bit of a perfectionist, so I really need to be sure of what I am making before I try and sell anything."

Ceramics, and building a business, require persistence and humility, she says. "We deal with a lot of failures in most steps of creating an object. Pieces break, kilns break—you have to start over many times to get things right. There are rewards and a lot of heartache. It is not about getting rich quickly or even making a moderate living for a while. It takes time to have your own style and have it actually be made well enough to sell."

It is also a lifestyle: "I am surrounded by pottery at home, I make pottery, I teach pottery, so I just can't really separate business from life. I find this to be common with other makers out there, too. I'm not sure if that is a good or bad thing!"

MEMORY, MEANING AND MOTIVATION

JULIE WHITMORE

Julie Whitmore makes a mean apple pie, and judging by the art she creates, it is a good bet that a cup of tea, a slice of that pie and an afternoon of conversation about her life and work would be a fairly memorable experience.

There is a freedom and joy in Julie's use of colour and material gestures in her work, and there is a richness to the narratives her work tells. Julie's ceramic works hover in that liminal space between function and sculpture. The surfaces of her cups, teapots and plates are magically filled with illustration and narrative. So much is contained in these surfaces that the illustrations often jump out onto the forms as sculpted animals, vegetables, figures and insects.

With so much story in Julie's work, one needs time to sit with her art and experience it. For many functional clay artists, that is where the art exists in their pottery: in the experience, the time spent with them and their use as an everyday object. Julie leads her viewer through narratives of human interaction with nature, through nostalgic times of abundance and through scenes filled with the joy of working and living on the land. The vibrancy of her illustrations allows you to almost smell the nearby sea air or hear the birds overhead. "My customer is the kind of person who feels the pull of the outdoors, who gets chills hearing the bark of a seal or the lapping of water," Julie says. "I am looking to connect to the viewer, to a place or a memory of a time in their life with meaning. I regularly paint animals, insects and vegetation to express our connection and need for communion with nature."

"In the morning when I wake I know I have just this one day. I think of this in terms of an opportunity I mustn't squander. I don't think about tomorrows or next week. So if it's just this one day, I had better get to work."

JULIE WHITMORE   41

UPBRINGING IN ART

Julie grew up in Orange County, California, her days filled with adventures similar to the scenes she represents on her pottery. She recalls a childhood of outdoor adventures, reading and of freedom. "I am grounded by nature, art and music. I was raised in a pink ranch house filled with paintings, books and smells of epicurean cooking. Jazz, classical or dreamy vocals issued forth from the stereo at all times. I remember digging in the backyard dirt and finding hunks of yellow clay. I loved the feel and texture of it. I marvelled at its malleable nature in the drier earth."

CAST OF CHARACTERS

Her work could be described as a modern interpretation of Rococo themes, but beneath all the joyous energy of Julie's work lie darker themes and narratives. Pull back the veil of the idyllic illustrations and you will see that some of the characters are not quite so naive or kind. Julie's portraits of women stare straight at you with strength and courage, their eyes pensive; these women are not here just to be looked at for their beauty. In some illustrations, women float protectively and dreamlike above the natural world. They carry whales and animals in their arms, and boats on their heads; they are telling you a tale, in whispers and in glances—a tale of danger lurking beyond the idyllic. Are the wolves poised to attack? Are those thunderclouds moving in? Where there are humans and nature, the scene is set for the drama to unfurl. The moral of her tales is that through harmony, respect and protection of the land, we can maintain a beautiful and sustainable life. Julie's work is moving toward more otherworldly surroundings. She will be adding to her cast of recurring characters. Her husband is represented by the whale, by the way, and she is present as the face of the moon, "casting what glow I am able."

"Success is
making *your* vision,
no one else's."

JULIE WHITMORE

STUDIO PROCESS

Play is integral to both the narrative of the work and to Julie's process in the studio. She starts her work with a loose sketch to cover the shape of the form and the elements that will potentially be sculpted. "Everything starts for me with the form," she says. "It will tell you what seems to sit just right on it, what is too much or not enough." That sketch will then move with her throughout the studio, to the potter's wheel and to the table where she hand-builds, directing her through each firing and addition of colour, glaze and luster. "I don't have a set palette. I have about 50 colours and I use all of them at different times. If I am trying to get a mood across—say, a melancholy one—I might use more blue and grey tones; for a joyous piece, lots of yellows."

ONE-WOMAN BUSINESS

Julie is a full-time ceramicist who finds sustainability in her business through selling her work online, bypassing the cut taken by galleries and shops. "I use an Instagram page to promote my pottery and announce upcoming listings, which I have at least twice a month," she says. "I list in groups of 10 to 12 pieces, twice a month. I take photos in the morning when the lighting is just right. I have an in-home studio and have taken over the garage and two rooms in the house. I pack everything at one time and use recycled shipping supplies." ✣

"I start with a sketch—sometimes rough, just a thought. I may think I want to make a handless cup that has a sensual feel and a reinforced base. A loose sketch. If it's a teapot, I will draw in much more detail, including the sculpted pull for the lid and the flowers I add. I will choose a poem stanza for the reverse. I pin the drawing up and refer to it as I throw, and then again later as I hand-build."

WORKSPACES

Julie's painting studio is bright, roomy and simple; a wall of windows and glass doors let the light spill in.

Her area for throwing and hand-building is large, "but never big enough," she says. "I have two electric kilns, a steel-headed wheel on legs, a rolling table. Two worktables. A good banding wheel. I don't use a lot of tools, but the ones I do use are like extensions of my hands."

In a typical workweek, she will spend one day throwing. "If the pieces are larger, I will trim them the next morning," she explains. "As I am already in the clay, I will move on to the rolling table. I'll make slabs for slump moulds of large bowls, platters, beakers."

Julie breaks for lunch and always has some tea or water handy. "Afternoons are good for cleaning up, getting ready for the next session." She sets aside a day or two for glazing. She photographs completed work in the morning, listing items for sale online in the evening. "I end the day," she says, "with a walk."

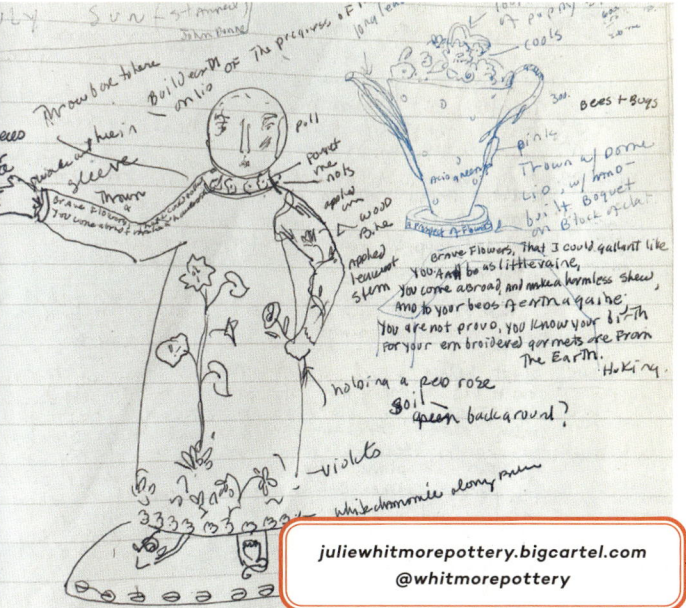

juliewhitmorepottery.bigcartel.com
@whitmorepottery

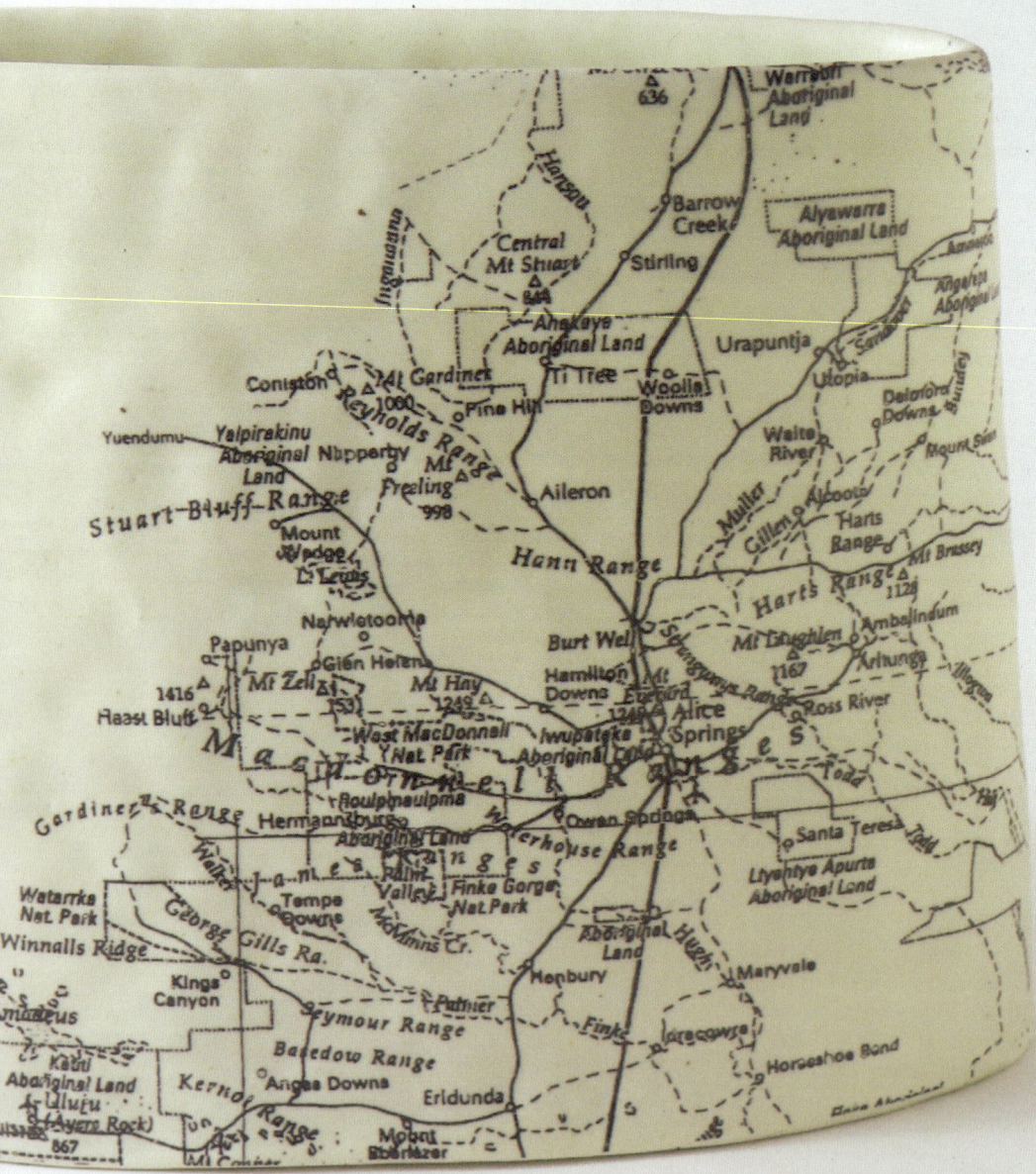

FINDING THE ESSENCE

MEL ROBSON

"I love the feeling of sitting at a wheel with a whole lot of clay ready to throw, or an empty ware board with the base of my next hand-built work waiting to be built, or an object to be cast. There is so much possibility in that beginning stage."

As an artist interested in exploring ideas of place, Mel Robson has definitely chosen to live in one of the most beautiful places: Alice Springs, Central Australia. She believes that identity and the ways in which histories, stories and associations are told can become embedded in everyday objects. These themes have always played a part in Mel's work—shifting with the landscape as she and her family moved from the lush and tropical bustling city of Brisbane to the arid outback of Australia. The move to Alice Springs in 2010 also broadened her practice. "It has expanded to include collaborative projects with the local community and a deeper focus on the ways in which people experience and represent place."

As a student and during her early post-grad years, Mel was focused on the utilitarian associations of the ceramic medium. "I liked the idea of making something you could use," she says. "But then I became really interested in the way these objects could be used to speak about things beyond function, the way stories can become embedded in objects—the narrative possibilities the material affords." While Mel has continued to work with functional objects, she has diversified her practice to include sculptures, site-specific installations, public art pieces and collaborative projects with local communities. Rather than being material-driven, Mel responds to the project idea she has in mind by researching and undertaking the best-suited process to create her vision. Mel spends significant amounts of time combing through archives or at the library researching.

Many visual references, all pulled from Mel's diverse interests, surface in her minimalist work. While her aesthetic might be paired down, her subject matter is rich in content and context. Through her research, she has come to include elements of textiles and material history in her work, as well as architecture, maps and cartography. She has also delved into aspects of ceramic history, exploring in particular her fascination with the traditions of blue-and-white ceramics. Her seemingly limitless passion for learning, she says, is what keeps her art practice playful and fun, rather than feeling like work.

REFERENCING THE NATURAL WORLD

Mel's work contains layers of coded references presented through a style that is uniquely her own. The beautiful, refined forms and smooth surfaces beg to be handled. In them she captures the vastness of a starry sky, the beauty of the cracked earth beneath one's feet, the sense of wonder of flying over a landscape and the play between the macro and miniature. Her objects are physical representations of the moments when we pause, appreciate, ponder and acknowledge our interconnectedness with the natural and man-made world around us.

LEARNING AS A TEACHER

Mel divides her time between teaching university-level ceramics and making in one of her two studios. "Teaching is a great reminder to play," she says. "I learn so much from my students—they're always coming up with different approaches that keep me excited and wondering! This is probably mostly because they don't know all the 'rules' yet, so they push things in ways you might not once you know more."

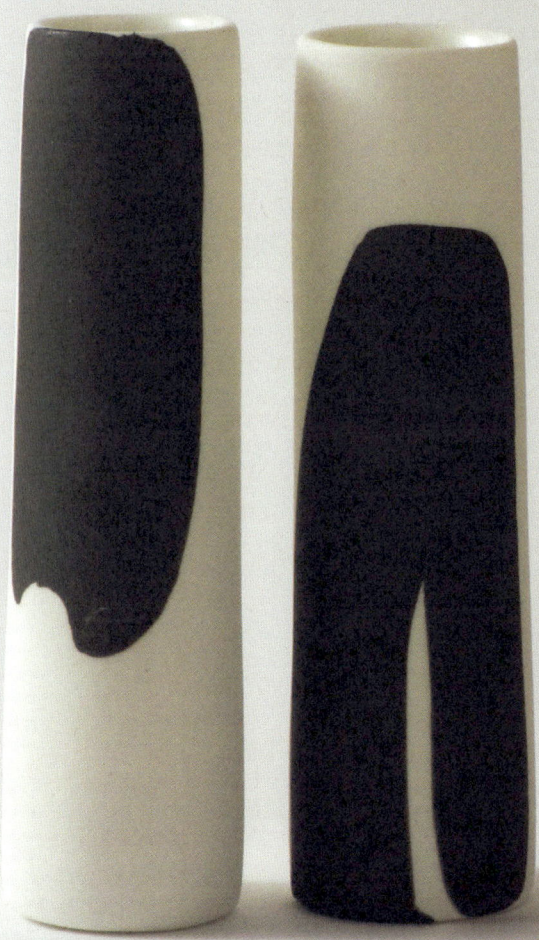

"I prefer not to use just one technique or one approach, but to move between functional and sculptural, installation and interactive, to put different processes next to each other and see how they speak to one another—found ceramic objects combined with handmade pieces, hand-built works alongside slip-cast objects, hand-drawn marks combined with digital imagery. I like the subtle variation of form and surface when combining objects made using different processes. Really it comes down to the story, the narrative I'm working with, and that determines the approach I take and the technique I use."

MINIMALIST STYLE

Mel describes her style as "fairly minimalist, restrained and pared back." She loves simplicity in form, as well as rich but simple surfaces. "I like to distill ideas down to their bare minimum," she says. "I use a monochromatic colour palette with an occasional splash of blue or the deep red of the local clay from where I live."

Through her work, Mel is always striving for simplicity and order, characteristics that she also desires in her own life—"but don't necessarily always achieve!" she admits. "It's a way of finding calm, to make sense of things in a way that is really visceral and tactile. In my work and my life, I think I'm always looking for the essence of something, the core or the truth, and so I tend to pare my work back to the barest essentials, to distill and try to discover what's left after that process, after everything extraneous is taken away. I am also really interested in people, in the ways we connect—or don't connect—with each other, so a lot of my work and projects are designed or made to engage with people on a fairly personal level, whether through a narrative or by using the material in a relational context—to create or facilitate connections." ✤

TWO STUDIOS

As she describes it, Mel's home studio is "a run-down old corrugated iron shed in my backyard with no lining and no air conditioning." The hot summers of the Australian outback make it virtually impossible to work in this studio, so she is lucky to also have use of the ceramic studio on campus, which is fully equipped and air-conditioned. The campus studio also provides a more communal environment in which to work during times when she is not focused, head down, on impending deadlines.

melrobson.com
@melrobsonceramics

SPIRIT AND SELF

AARON CALDWELL

Working out of the ceramic studio at Illinois State University, Aaron Caldwell is partway through his master's studies in art education. There is a good reason why he is focusing on both art education and ceramics: it is related to his upbringing. "My interests in life have always revolved around education improvements in communities that resemble the community I grew up in," Aaron says. "College has allowed me to tap into my artistic side, which led me to discover my interest in art education, engagement and making in Black, Brown and queer communities."

Aaron has not been working in ceramics very long. "I took my first ceramic class in the fall of 2016, which was my third year as an education major. A friend of mine recommended the class to me. I quickly took an interest in the medium because I saw the potential of hand-building. Prior to ceramics, I only knew about painting and drawing." It was a defining moment. "Taking ceramics opened my eyes to the art world."

The versatility of clay has kept him passionate about his ceramic pursuits. "It's a material that can easily become what I want it to become, whether that is two-dimensional, three-dimensional, functional, sculptural, imitative, interactive or temporary."

In the studio, you will find Aaron creating highly researched and thematically rich narrative works. He draws from historical references such as the material histories of the minkisi (a spirit, or the object a spirit inhabits) of the Kongo people (from present-day Angola), as well as contemporary content pulled from his own experiences and those of his communities. Historical artwork both in and outside of ceramics

"My work is primarily influenced by work that has been around for centuries. I look to traditional works from the Black diaspora like the Kongo people's minkisi and African American folk art like quilts and baskets."

inspires this young artist, who is constantly looking to push the boundaries and expectations of the medium.

"FAUX POTS"

Aaron makes sculptural pieces that reference functional vessel forms, but which have had that function removed. "I came across this idea of 'faux pots' because I really enjoyed looking at decorative pots from various cultures," he says. "Their vessels, plates and varying pots were all functional. However, I did not enjoy the decorative pots for their function, but for the decorative aspect." Aaron omits the functional aspect from his work so that content and narrative are at the forefront. "People would essentially have to submit to the idea of enjoying my pots for their visual elements instead of thinking of what kind of flowers or liquid to put in my pots."

The narratives Aaron brings to his work come from his observations of the language, fashion, entertainment and cultural experiences of his communities. Recent pieces combine human hair with sculpted combs on the sculptures. Gloopy glaze applied in repeating surface patterns becomes a visually compelling design element, as well as looking like lotion. He uses the reference to beauty products to speak of the elders in his life who reinforced the beauty of his skin by telling him "that the sun loved us and blessed us with our beautiful skin colour because we have melanin in our skin. In other words, we were always told that we were sun-kissed."

SURFACE INSPIRATION

Aaron's visual style has been influenced by two-dimensional art practices such as painting and textiles. "The painting medium is important to my ceramic work," he explains. "Since painting is the most

"My work stems from experiences that I have had as a Black gay person, and I want to make work that gives those Black and/or gay folk more opportunities to see aspects of our lives reflected in artwork. And because my work speaks to and of similar experiences my demographic may find relatable, it creates an opportunity for non-Black and non-queer people to learn something new about other people or even themselves."

accessible medium and visibly relevant work in art history and the contemporary, I have spent a lot of time looking at Black painters." Two of his favourite artists are Aaron Douglas, the highly regarded muralist known for addressing racial issues in America through representing the African American community, and Alma Thomas, the expressionist painter who broke down barriers through her career for women artists of colour. "When I make work with more imagery-based narrative, I feel Aaron Douglas' influence comes through by my decision to make distinctive solid blocks of colour to create my imagery. Alma Thomas' influence comes into play in my building process mark-making and the way I decorate my work with the lotion glaze. Her repetitive mark-making and colour choices to guide the viewer's eyes around her piece are what I strive to do in my work. I also am inspired by Gee's Bend quilters and how they strive to keep their spontaneous nature in decision making at the forefront of quilting. I keep this in mind when making decisions in my work."

"There seems to be a huge push on experimentation of what the medium can be with clay and with glaze, which has led to a lot of amazing discoveries by contemporary artists. This has inspired me to consider how I am pushing the medium in my own work. I begin to consider how I use the clay and how I use the glaze to create a new experience for viewers—that's where I fit into the picture of contemporary ceramics."

STUDIO

Aaron works the clay quickly in the building process to emphasize a sense of energy flowing through his pieces. His biggest consideration is in highlighting the evidence of human interaction with material. "My aesthetic is evident-based building, so you see the direction my hands went when I smoothed out the coils, where my fingers pressed into the clay. I want my work to give the viewer a sense of how I built it, whether that means they know I coil-build because they see a glimpse of the inside of my work and notice the defining coils, or the pace or direction my hands went when smoothing out the outside, or where my fingers pressed into the clay to shape the piece. My work consistently has steel nails in it, so when it comes to firing I do not go past cone one, and try to limit each piece to two firings. I keep my processes simple and straightforward because content matters to me more than technique or process." Aaron works with a red-brown stoneware clay that can be fired to a higher temperature than similar-coloured low-temperature earthenware clays. He underfires this cone six clay body to get a bright "toasty red."

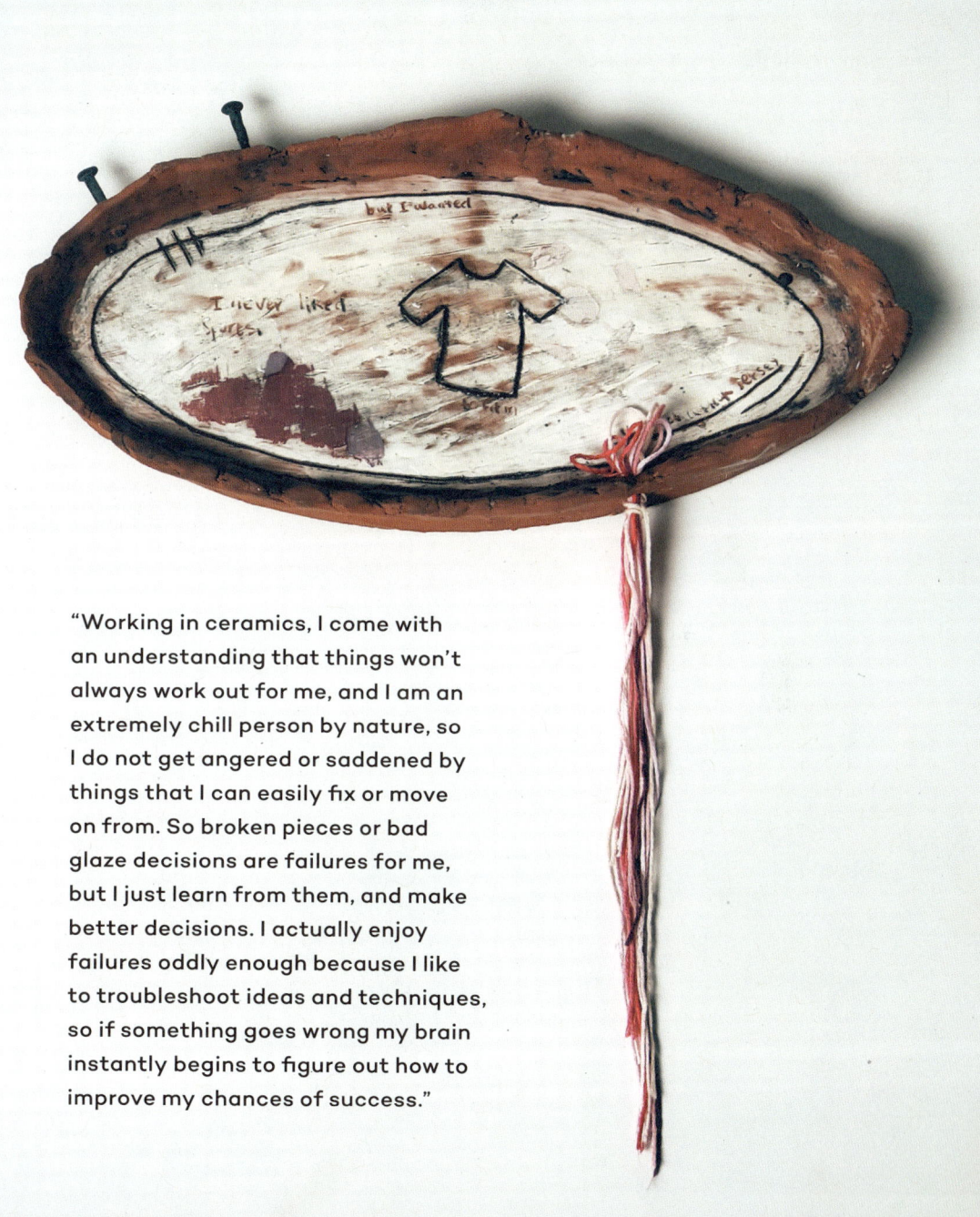

"Working in ceramics, I come with an understanding that things won't always work out for me, and I am an extremely chill person by nature, so I do not get angered or saddened by things that I can easily fix or move on from. So broken pieces or bad glaze decisions are failures for me, but I just learn from them, and make better decisions. I actually enjoy failures oddly enough because I like to troubleshoot ideas and techniques, so if something goes wrong my brain instantly begins to figure out how to improve my chances of success."

FUTURE GOALS

Aaron hopes to find a career helping to diversify the ceramics field, with an emphasis on art accessibility in underrepresented communities. "A lot of times, making visual art as a hobby or a professional career can be viewed as a 'White' thing, so the communities I connect with are a lot of times the places where art spaces do not exist or target," he says. "Ultimately, I am interested in doing the necessary work, whether that be in one community or several." Currently, Aaron works a gallery job that gives him the opportunity to expand his experiences in outreach and art education. He also teaches art to youth through a nonprofit organization. "I hope to continue to learn from these jobs to then take the lessons learned with me, so I can continue similar work elsewhere. If I can continue the work after these two years, then that would be my definition of success." ✻

ceramicsnstuff.com
@ceramicsnstuff

TALES OF RESILIENCE

JAPNEET KAUR

The rich poetry of Japneet Kaur's work is an indication of how much of her own life and experiences she brings to the narratives in her work. Japneet makes illustration-based ceramics out of her studio in Toronto, Ontario. The long journey that brought her to Canada is woven into the drawings for which her work is known. These are stories of family, love, turmoil, culture, loss and renewal.

"I was born in Punjab, surrounded by the comfort and security of family, where my home grew near a pond that was lined with milkweed and shone with the sparkle of kingfishers," describes Japneet. "The pond sung with the choruses of water buffaloes, frogs and crickets, and at night fireflies studded the pond's dark blanket with dazzling displays. As I grew, this pond was paved over by development but remained central to my fond memories of growing up during a time of a rapidly changing physical and socio-political landscape."

She was pursuing a degree in fine arts when tragedy struck her family. "Just after graduating, my life's flow was suddenly interrupted when my father violently passed away in 2003. The safe nest of my home was swept away, tossing me into a turbulent journey of overcoming loss, leaving my home and trying to build a new one."

Japneet's journey with clay began in 2005, but had to be put on hold when she immigrated to Toronto the following year. Once in Canada, she felt she had to follow "the more accepted narrative of an immigrant life," Japneet explains. "I bid goodbye to art and started on a path of making for myself a more practical and predictable life." Burnout ensued and Japneet came to

"For me the power of art is that it blurs boundaries. Its doors and windows are open for anyone to enter, as each story is precious and adds to the fabric of the collective story of our time."

"I grew up surrounded by people whose hands were always making things—knitting warmth, pickling summer and making chutneys, embroidering lush gardens of thread onto hand-stitched dresses and textiles. As children we were often given bits and pieces of material to work with alongside the adults. I have many warm memories of sitting with my Biji (grandmother) and learning from her to knit. I also remember hand-painting bouquets of flowers on bedsheets and pillow covers with my mom and forming tiny birds out of the dough that she used to make roti."

realize that trying to assimilate to her new environment was not what she needed. She needed to speak her story and value her unique contribution to the world.

Japneet took ceramic classes again and now fills her days with stories and characters, life and beauty. Her art practice also includes painting, drawing and stop motion animation. The theme of journeys, which has always been a part of her narrative, is woven through those mediums as well. Drawn characters move off the page and interact in stop motion with flowers from the garden in a dance and a tale of joy and resilience.

WHAT WAS LEFT IS NOT LOST

Japneet generously and honestly shares her memories of the life she had to leave behind. Ceramics were a part of her everyday life during her childhood, and today she takes these remnants of the distinct cultural use of ceramics and reinterprets them in different clay bodies, in a new country, surrounded by different cultural influences.

Japneet recalls the sweltering summers of Punjab: "Terracotta clay vessels (gharas) were used abundantly to keep water cool and also filtered. One could also find community gharas strung around the streets for thirsty passersby. Small terracotta cups were also used by local sweet sellers to sell tea and yogurt. Wide terracotta platters were filled to the brim for birds to take a dip for respite from the burning sun. These were my first connections to clay being used for function, mostly red terracotta."

As she grew older, she became aware of her grandmother's tiny cupboard. "It hung in the dining room, full of her coveted collection of china and porcelain cups, saucers and kettles," she recalls. "These were kept away from our careless, tiny hands and would only get aired out on very special occasions. I have

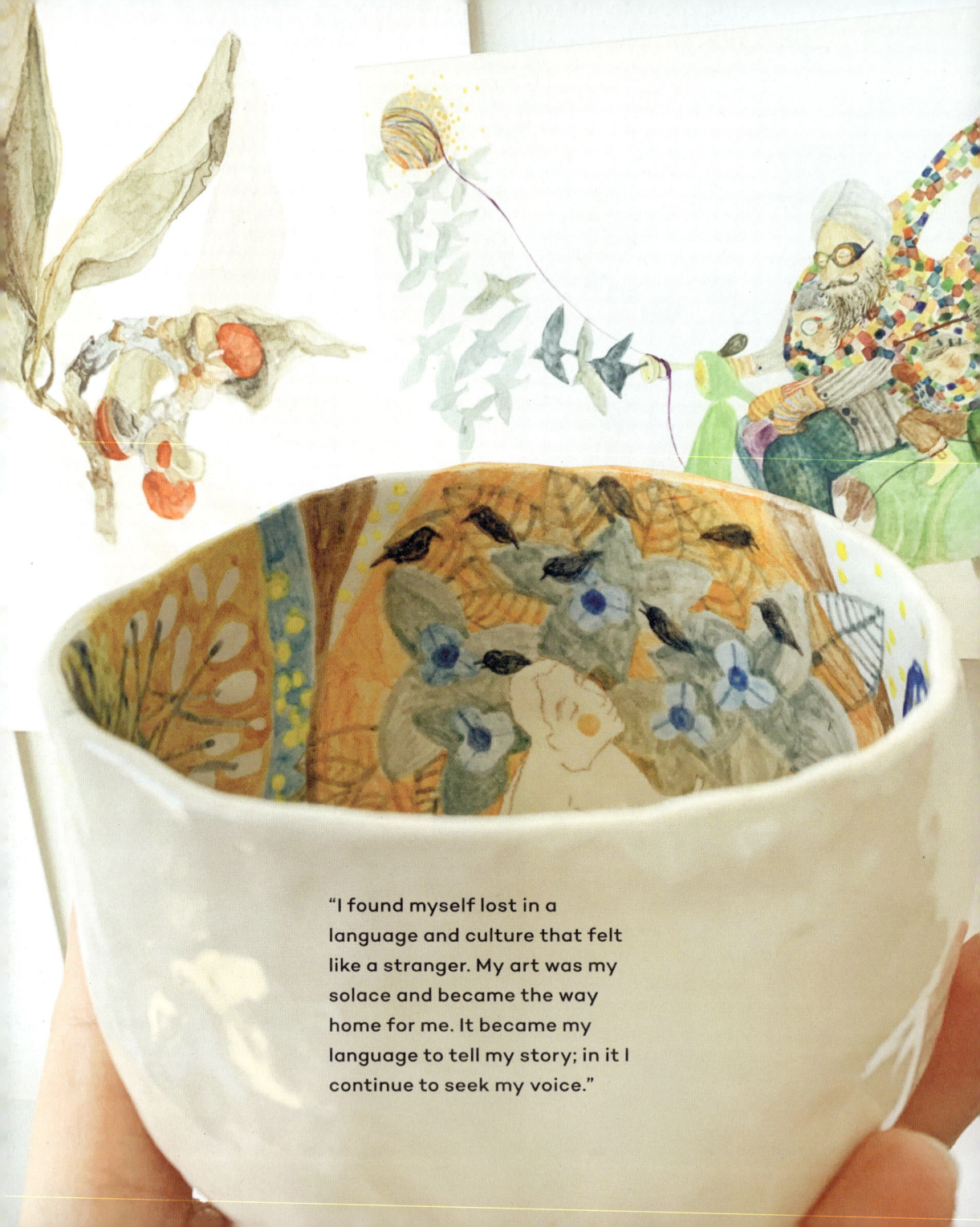

"I found myself lost in a language and culture that felt like a stranger. My art was my solace and became the way home for me. It became my language to tell my story; in it I continue to seek my voice."

spent many afternoons, along with my sister, climbing on chairs to reach these treasures as the adults in the house retired to have a siesta. The glitter of the gold on the cup lip and handles, beautiful delicate bouquets blooming on a background of translucent porcelain from their bell-like forms, the graceful spouts shaped like a peacock's neck! To hold them and play with them for a precious few minutes was well worth the risk of climbing over rickety chairs and was probably when I fell in love with the beauty and functionality of pottery and ceramics."

THREADS OF HUMANITY

Japneet's pieces draw in their viewer, requesting both time and thoughtful consideration. They beckon to be held in order to share the story held within; they want you as a viewer to relate to them and to weave your own narrative into them, like a conversation. "My drawings on the pottery are visual images of what is close to my heart," she says. "They are tiny gardens that grow on the bisqued forms from tiny kernels of stories that the world around me scatters in my lap. My work is my process of understanding and tuning in through the thickets of endless chatter to the things that matter to me: robust ecosystems, healthy communities, vibrant hives, safe sanctuaries, webs of reciprocity. Habitats that embrace and do not *other*. It dreams of delicate threads of humanity and the natural world weaving into one another, into a fabric rich in diversity and mutual respect—congregations of caring circles knitting pods of safety around each other."

JAPNEET KAUR

"My work is all hand-formed using hand-pinching and moulds. I use the surface of my vessels as a canvas to draw and paint upon. I have developed a palette and drawing technique over time that suits both the drawing and painting mediums and that complement the surface of the clay."

OTHER MAKERS THAT INSPIRED

Japneet's formative years were spent surrounded by makers; consequently, the character of the maker is often seen in her work—such as the knitter whose textile curls and drapes, and ebbs and flows like a river through her pieces. The knitter is a particularly eloquent metaphor for time and space, journeying and care.

Japneet received a fine art degree from the Chandigarh College of Arts in Punjab, but it was in her own community and culture where she was taught her most valuable lessons. Memories of hand-painting flowers on bedsheets with her mother, or "embroidering lush gardens of thread onto hand-stitched dresses and textiles," are the memories of creative lessons that she holds most dear. As a child she was included in creative work alongside the adults; scraps of materials passed her way for her to experiment with and learn on. The patterning of flowers in her illustrations draws from those memories and skills she learned in her youth. ✻

storyofaseed.com
@storyofaseed

JAPNEET'S ADVICE FOR LIFE AND ART

It takes time to grow a business; be patient. Pace yourself. Remember it's not a race.

Have a clear vision of what is important for you to say, and stay authentic to this as much as you can. Remember what inspired you to start, and reconnect with this often.

Respect your journey and that of others. Do not compare; we all have our paths and challenges—keep walking on yours, one small step at a time.

Keep yourself open, offer and seek support and try to build a community of support. Walk in good company.

Find small joys in what you do and in your day. Make the process enjoyable.

Keep a journal of positive experiences as reminders when the going gets tough.

Don't get stuck in labels; experiment, play, learn and share.

There will be failures; see them as seeds for reflection and growth.

IMAGINATION MADE REAL

MARINE BOSSU

Outside Marine Bossu's studio, light moves across the garden, highlighting the olive trees in the surrounding French countryside and pouring into the large windows where she works. "In front of the main table I work on, there is a French window, so I just need to raise my head to look at nature," she says. "It really gives me inspiration every day."

Marine belongs to a lineage of practicing artists that includes her artist grandmother and her craftsman father, who was skilled in making frames. Her beautiful studio was once her father's workshop, and her desire to create and engage with the world through art has been a deeply rooted part of her everyday life since childhood. "As a very stressful child, art gave me some sort of internal peace, a lovely way to escape from reality. Art was my daily dose of happiness, so as soon as I could, I went to an art school."

Growing up in Salernes, a small potters' village internationally known for *tomettes* (hexagonal tiles made of red terracotta), Marine could hardly escape the pull towards clay. As early as grade school, she was introduced to pottery through lessons by a local artist; years later, she worked in the atelier of Anne-Laure, a mentor who not only expanded Marine's studio practice but her professional practice as well. This training is what led Marine to switch from studying graphic design and illustration to studying ceramics—computer-based illustration lacked a tactile element that she craved, and which was satiated with clay. "I drew a lot when I was young, and it was a way for me to tell my own stories," she says. "Drawing only in 2D was really frustrating to me. I needed volume, consistency."

"People say that my work is filled with poetry and tenderness. Every day becomes lighter, with fantasy and gentleness all around. This is all I can hope for. I heal my soul while creating objects I love, and it makes me happy."

There is a strong aesthetic sensibility and style to her work, in which can be seen the influence not only of traditional Chinese and Japanese ceramic techniques but also of contemporary pop culture, with references to the films of Hayao Miyazaki and Studio Ghibli. "Miyazaki is one of the biggest influences in my life and work," Marine says. "He does not only create beautiful movies; he is sharing an ideology and an ecological value that can touch people directly in their hearts."

THE YOUNG COLLECTOR

Marine has been a collector since she was young, collecting objects of all shapes and forms. "I like picking up small wooden sticks, shells on the beach, small glass bottles, dried grass, pieces of fabric," she says. "All my drawers are full of little things I collect and cherish. Their shapes, forms, colours and textures inspire me. It's a bit like before Pinterest existed. Sometimes I pick something randomly out of my treasure box and use it for inspiration for my ceramics. For example, my travellers are holding small glass bottles as backpacks, dried grass in their hands. They are even using shells as hiding spots."

"Contemporary ceramics is a type of ceramic that uses ancestral skills without restricting itself to codes, by pushing back the limits of the material in order to exploit and experiment with new things."

THE TRAVELLER

Stories wind their way throughout Marine's functional pottery, giving life to a repeating character who plays out her stories on beautiful everyday objects intended for use in the home. Her "Traveller" character also jumps off the drawn surface into small sculptures that she documents in equally compelling scenes and photographs. "Little by little, my work started to touch a lot of different people, and it was such a surprise," she says. "Children, teenagers, young parents, elderly persons. In fact, the stories I tell are universal. This character who I use a lot in my ceramics is a kind guardian of nature, of the living. He is a symbol of our common beliefs. My illustrations can reconnect everyone to their inner child." Universal narratives seem to nestle into Marine's work, and be perfectly at home there. The Traveller seeks out adventure, engages with nature, nurtures relationships and meditates in solitude. It is as if he embodies our dreams for our futures, our joy in the everyday and our nostalgia for past experiences.

"My wildest dream was to give life to my own characters, so they'd become real. Clay's magical power is to give a bit of life into something; it gives a soul to the creations we make."

ONLINE BUSINESS

"I love to work late at night, so I use my morning for other things," Marine says: "taking pictures for my website or Instagram, thinking of my next post, writing captions under my post, working on my Instagram story… In general, I always write several posts in advance." Marine understands the value of creating an audience online for a viable studio practice. The beautiful narrative branding of her social media flawlessly matches the aesthetics of her work, demonstrating her refined business know-how. Her background in graphic design also comes to play in her marketing style. "You must highlight your work, know how to sell your creations and how to maintain good customer relationships in order to gain popularity. You really need a lot of different skills to survive competition. But I must say that this is what I love about my job. There is a lot to do, a lot to achieve and to understand—you never get bored." ❖

"All the love I try to give through my work comes back to me like a boomerang when one single person tells me they fell in love with my art."

marinebossu.com
@marine.bossu

STUDIO

Marine uses traditional methods in her studio such as the slab-built or the coil and pinch techniques used by Yixing potters when making their famous teapots. She learned these techniques firsthand during travels abroad. "This technique really moved me, so I want to continue making those small teapots using my own talent," she says.

The simple, handmade tools of these artists resonate with her and are instrumental to the style of forms she produces. However, whenever Marine can, she bypasses any tool and works directly with her hands. For her, the immediacy of the stoneware clay at her fingertips sparks a connection with the material and brings her utter joy. Teapots, serving dishes, cups and vases are all a part of her functional repertoire, but the teapot is perhaps the most sacred, as it brings her back to that experience of learning from the Yixing teapot makers, and with it the weight of the history attached to that experience.

"Collaborative pieces help us break outside of our routines and force us to make decisions differently."

DIVING DEEP

LYNNE HOBAICA & RICKIE BARNETT

Lynne Hobaica and Rickie Barnett work out of their shared studio in the Blue Ridge Mountains of western North Carolina, in Bakersville. The studio is a hop, skip and a jump up the hill from their home. For two young artists working out the balance of art and life, each having day jobs to sustain their studio practice, it is crucial to have the studio close at hand. After a long workday, Lynne and Rickie can sit down together for dinner and then enjoy their shared passion for clay until the wee hours of the morning. "It's a modest building of about 300 square feet, but it's perfect for us," Rickie says. "Lynne and I each have our own worktables and we have a shared table for rolling slabs and spreading out. There's a tool area by the sink, a kiln in the corner, a bunch of shelves, some plants, a stack of clay and some plastic dinosaurs." Rickie says it is his favourite place in the world—which might also be because his most beloved person is there with him.

"Our collaborations are very playful in their creation. This playfulness spills over into our own practices and keeps things fun and fresh."

"Through all of our difficult and traumatic experiences, it can be easy to feel worn, battered and like giving up. I choose to find joy in every moment, searching for a purpose to move forward, to appreciate what is in our lives. That is why I choose to make art every day, and that is what helps me move forward in the most challenging times."
—Lynne

FAMILY NARRATIVE

Rickie grew up in Northern California in a family that he describes as having "the distinction of being both extremely religious and hard-working poor." Lynne was born one state over in Arizona to a large family of six children that she describes as "a family of explosive laughers." They met through mutual friends at a national ceramics conference, the National Council on Education for the Ceramic Arts (NCECA), and within three months the collaborative creative spark was ignited. Lynne and Rickie were already known for their individual creative practices, so they named their new collaborative project Two Headed Diver. Each artist has a distinct aesthetic and technical approach to working in clay, but both hold steadfast to their work involving illustrative, narrative-based functional pottery and sculptures.

DRAWING AS COPING STRATEGY

These two storytellers work in clay to express the rich world of human emotions. Rickie's narratives evolve from his childhood, in which he was witness to extreme poverty alongside religious fanaticism. "Drawing became my way of dealing with the struggles of this collision of worlds," he says. "It became my way of exploring the desolate landscape of tension and conflicting emotions. My work has always been driven from this point of reference." In his youth he witnessed "the heavy nature of living in a part of town filled with drugs, mental illness and backwoods mindsets." Lynne's work is also autobiographical, layering both the light and dark sides of the human condition. "I'm often pulling from relationships and interactions with people or animals for my imagery," she says. "My hope, however, is that others can look at the work and find their own stories and connections to it."

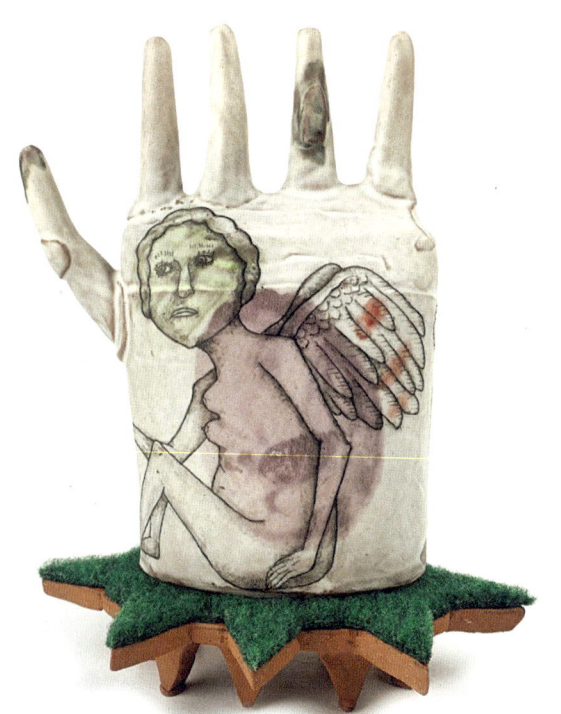

SCULPTURAL PURSUITS

Both Lynne and Rickie rely more on the functional pottery to pay the bills, but they derive particular fulfillment from the sculptural work they undertake. Rickie feels "a greater sense of pleasure and growth from working sculpturally. The sculptures let me unpack more narrative into them, resulting in me unpacking more of myself." Regardless of whether it is on a cup or a sculpture, Rickie says, "the most important thing for me, in my work, is the narrative. I make work because I want to tell stories. Using functional ware to portray some of these narratives gives me the opportunity to share these stories within other people's homes. It's important to me to be able to let this work live in the homes of others, and the functional work lends itself to letting that be possible for people who aren't in a financial place to spend thousands of dollars on a useless sculpture."

LAYERED NARRATIVES

Lynne finds the process of creating functional work to be laid back, spontaneous and playful. All of this play and experimentation shows up in her labour-intense and finely detailed sculptures. "In both my sculptural and functional work, the part that I find most compelling is the drawing," she says. "I don't usually have a plan before a piece is finished; rather, I create elements that I can have a conversation with in my drawing, such as with form or blocks of colour." At first glance, Lynne's drawings appear charming; they are colourful, eccentric, somewhat familiar and nostalgic. But they are also layered with characters and scenes that tell tales of existential conflict. "I am inspired by the beauty and struggle of the stories we experience, often locating humour in moments that were once painful or embarrassing. Through colour and form, my work dances in a world of play, deep emotion and empathy."

"The power of storytelling is learning about other people's perspectives and growing in empathy. By sharing my stories in my work, I am hopeful that my work will reach beyond people with a background similar to mine and connect us at a deeper level."
—Lynne

EMOTIONS DISGUISED AS PLAY

Rickie's works feel like a well-loved object; they look weathered and worn, embedded with the aesthetic of the patina of use. The same could be said of the characters he creates. Each of their illustrated faces portray the years of experience that compose a life. "I create characters based on the struggle of balancing relationships," he says. "I place them in an open-ended narrative where they can explore emotions that have been experienced but not quite understood. Objects such as childhood toys, musical instruments, animals and old household items, all lend themselves to conveying heavy emotions, disguised as the act of play." ✽

"My favourite tool is our kiln. It was expensive, it's shiny and new, and our entire practice relies on it—not to mention that it looks like a little robot sitting in the corner. Whenever I'm having a hard day, I remind myself that I own a little robot that can transform a material's physical properties in its tiny little hellish belly, and that maybe I'm not doing so bad in life."
—Rickie

BUSINESS

In terms of good business practice, Rickie offers the following advice: "Being able to be honest with yourself about your limits and mental health, helps in the pursuit of persistence, which I believe is among the most important traits for building a business. Being curious about business and talking to others about how they are approaching or solving problems in their business has been a tremendous benefit."

Lynne's day job as the finance coordinator at the Penland Gallery allows her to understand the give and take of an artist/gallery relationship from both sides. "There are several galleries that I have worked with over the years, and a few I have been honoured to stick by. Having open, honest conversations with a gallery about my expectations of them and their expectations of me is essential. ... I expect that they are working as hard to promote and sell the work as I am to create high-quality, engaging and thoughtful work."

VICKI GRIMA

NATURE

WRITTEN BY
JULIA KRUEGER

FROM PLANTS TO POTS

MORGAN DOANE

Plants, ceramics and the home have all had a long history together: Egyptians brought plants into their inner courts for display, Roman villas were scented with the blossoms of citrus trees, and in Tudor times, plants were regularly brought into more "modest" English homes. As plants made their way into the domestic sphere, ceramic pots of all shapes and sizes were created. In the late 18th century, for example, the stoneware manufacturer Wedgwood even had a "Flowerpot Room" where cornucopias as well as root, essence and bough pots were prominently on display. Considering this long history, it is no surprise that Morgan Doane of Tampa, Florida, a self-professed "plant lady," took up ceramics in order to create plant-centric pots for the home—because if you like plants, then you must also pay close attention to their "homes."

"I came into ceramics through my love of plants," Morgan explains. "Having the right vessel for my beloved greenery makes photography and display much more fun. I travelled to Colombia several years ago and fell in love with the simple terracotta pots I saw there and decided to come home and learn how to make them myself. I took classes for about a year at a local pottery studio before getting a wheel and kiln at my home." Having found it difficult to source quality, handmade pots with adequate drainage, Morgan turned to designing and making pots with attached saucers and drainage holes. In addition to her pottery work, Morgan co-wrote a book in 2018 with Erin Harding titled *How to Raise a Plant and Make it Love You Back*, and the two also started a "community for houseplant enthusiasts" on Instagram called @houseplantclub.

"My goal is to continue having fun. I'm not looking to become a famous ceramicist or open a gallery. I love making functional pieces that people find attractive enough to place their plants in. That's all I want to do."

"I trust my gut to keep experimenting and coming up with fun and cute ways to spruce up my planters."

Making pots for "plant people" is important to Morgan. She sells her work mainly through Etsy to "all the plant people out there who don't want to have to drill their own drainage holes in expensive, store-bought, mass-produced planters. I try to vary the glazing to fit within different types of décor." In addition to the white-speckled "heart of gold" pots, the funfetti-glazed pieces and drippy intergalactic pots, Morgan also creates hanging unglazed terracotta pots and a line of raku ware. For the hanging pots, she ties all the cording: "That often takes me an entire evening and has caused a callous or two." For her raku pieces, Morgan makes the pots, and her husband, Brian, raku-fires them in their garage.

Raku pottery originated in Japan in the 16th century as a way to create vessels for tea ceremonies, and the process was taken up by American potters in the 1950s. During the firing process, red hot pots are removed from the kiln and placed into a lidded receptacle filled with combustible organic materials such as sawdust, straw or newspaper. These materials

"The form that I make most frequently is a pot with an integral saucer attached. Each pot has drainage holes so that when you water your plant, the excess can drain out and get caught in the saucer. This helps prevent root rot and promotes healthier plants."

quickly burn away and the reduction atmosphere causes metallic flashing and black soot stain. The process is somewhat unpredictable and quick in comparison to many other firing processes, and this is part of its appeal. As Morgan explains, raku is "very time intensive—having to babysit the pieces until they are at the perfect temperature to pull from the kiln. But the process is also fun and I love that my husband is so involved and inspired. It was his idea to try raku, because he thought it would be fun to learn and experiment with. He loves experimenting with things, and the more dangerous the better." Her fiery, black raku pieces also appeal to her customers: "Those pieces are always the first to sell!"

Plants are at the core of Morgan's practice and she plans to continue getting her hands dirty in both the mud and dirt. "I'm going to keep working with clay as long as it's fun. I love that I have the wheel and kiln at home, so if I'm having a stressful day, I can always go outside on our covered porch and throw a few pieces to some wonderful music. It makes me forget about everything else when my hands are covered in mud." ❖

"I feel like a bit of an outsider in the field of contemporary ceramics because what I do is so niche. I admire so many artists' work and wish I had started on my ceramics journey earlier in life but I'm so grateful it's part of my life now. I never considered myself an artist before, but making pottery really allows me to see a different part of myself."

AN "OUTDOOR" STUDIO

Morgan's home studio is located alongside her pool in a screened-in lanai (porch), which is also conveniently close to her clay supply store. Her studio is equipped with a Brent wheel and an Olympic electric kiln. The lanai allows Morgan to feel like she is outdoors while still being sheltered by a roof and screen. It also allows her to be surrounded by plants and chirping birds. Because her studio is somewhat open to the elements, a typical day in the studio for Morgan changes with the seasons. In summer, when the heat becomes too much, she works in the evenings when it is cooler and glazes in the early mornings, "when the birds are chirping and the heat of the day hasn't settled in yet."

plantingpink.com
@plantingpink

B PRACTICAL POTTERY

BRIDGET FAIRBANK

Bridget Fairbank's ceramics practice has taken her to many places, from earning a diploma in clay in 2008 at the Kootenay School of the Arts in Nelson, British Columbia, in 2008, to a bachelor of fine art at the Nova Scotia School of Art and Design in Halifax, Nova Scotia, in 2013, to a master of fine arts at the University of Florida in Gainesville, Floria, in 2017, along with numerous residencies. Over time, her focus has shifted from functional wares to ceramic installations and ceramic-related happenings, often exploring themes of nature, food and human relationships. "I use the metaphorical landscapes of food and flora to make work that mediates our relationships," Bridget explains. "I consider flora, wild and domestic, as a living witness to intimate life. My art is plant-like, vibrant and plentiful—a reminder that we are not apart from nature. Pieces are conduits through which you may feel that growth is possible."

Not all work within the field of ceramics is focused exclusively on form or process—some artists create work that is focused instead on context, motion and interaction. Curator Alun Graves describes this as the expanded field of ceramics, in which individual objects have given way to ensembles, site and context are particularly important and time is of the essence. These ceramic objects or installations might only exist for a certain period of time or might undergo some type of change, all of it relating to performative or relational moments in which objects, audience and maker become "active participants." Bridget's practice is firmly rooted within this expanded field of ceramics, with work that assembles multiple parts into a whole, and installations that purposefully implicate her audience.

"Nature is attractive and craved by everyone. The gallery space, where my work is most often presented, is a place where people engage open-mindedly and expect to be challenged. The subject matter of my work is relevant in a world of climate change and a seductive reminder that daily actions matter. People need that."

For example, in 2015, Bridget explored the subject of the still life by carefully arranging her pottery alongside objects related to Florida's food industry, for her series *Natura Morta: A Florida Still Life*. Viewers were invited to smell the fresh soil, grass and citrus fruits in relation to symbols of death (skulls and taxidermy) and industry (tools and products), while contemplating how Florida's food industries have shaped the state's culture and landscape. A year later, she created *The Pineapple Project*, in which she designed specific ceramic stands for pineapples that allowed their juices to be optimally distributed throughout the fruit. She placed her ceramic stands on a table and invited gallery visitors to ponder the pineapple both physically (by cutting it open) and mentally (in terms of its history and production). For *Foodscapes: From Seed to Mouth*, Bridget encouraged viewers to harvest actual food from a ceramic, tile-based vertical garden that she made and to then prepare and eat a meal with her in the gallery. The exhibit encouraged actions surrounding gardening, planting, picking, preparing and eating, using them as gateways into discussions about food production and consumption.

Bridget's more recent work has focused on plant forms, creating plants that do not always exactly resemble their real-life counterparts. She often works quickly in series and will adjust and change her focus as needed, as she finds that one experiment or idea tends to lead to another. She sketches her ideas on paper or transparencies and then builds her work using moulds or slabs. For her larger pieces, Bridget designs them so that they are made up of many smaller parts, each made separately and then assembled together into a larger whole. This process is important to Bridget, not only because it is a practical way to work when your studio is constantly on the move, but because the kiln is no longer her endpoint: "The kiln for me does

BRIDGET FAIRBANK

"I believe the handcrafted object is now the subversive object. My objects act sometimes as objects of irony, sometimes as objects of intimacy and sometimes as a means to an educational end. I use the metaphorical landscapes of food and flora to make work that mediates our relationships. I consider flora, wild and domestic, as a living witness to intimate life. My art is plant-like, vibrant and plentiful—a reminder that we are not apart from nature. Pieces are conduits through which you may feel that growth is possible."

not mean an object is done. Fire does not have the last say. I get to compose, rearrange or even make a section of a piece again or create a whole new element to attach after firing." After firing, Bridget assembles her pieces using construction adhesives, finding that this way of working also enables her to edit at the installation phase, which can lead to "fresher objects." She also finds that writing about her ideas while making her pieces helps her refocus and adjust her work. She appreciates the process of critique, she says, as it requires her to explain herself in a different way.

Bridget's assembling of small parts into a larger whole is akin to growth, like a small patch of weeds turning into something much more substantial. For Bridget, her plant forms serve as conduits for communicating the idea that growth is possible and for fostering within the viewer an attentiveness to nature and an understanding of the important role

"Clay is a very special, malleable, archival material that can be used to address any topic on Earth and connect you to any time and place in human history. There is a lifetime of discovery within the medium."

that plants play within it, whether it be in an urban, rural or domestic environment. "Canadian wildfires, climate change, consumption in a globalized capital economy, land management, food production and feminism are core themes in my work and daily existence," she says. Her work conveys her conviction that plants are living witnesses to humanity, and the relational aspect of her practice is meant to prompt questions and foster an awareness of how people can be, and are, a part of nature rather than something apart from it. "Vibrant and boisterous work is my reaction to a dark and contemplative world view," she explains. "It is a reminder that growth is possible when paired with positive daily action." ✻

bpracticalpottery.com
@bpracticalpottery

"Ceramics does not give me peace of mind; it is a process that fuels my mind."

A NOMADIC STUDIO

"It is almost unimaginable to make a living on art making alone," says Bridget. "The diversification and creativity colleagues put into funding their art practices is staggering and I believe it helps make the ceramics world so varied and interesting—the side hustle is real. Having a diverse income stream only makes sense for my work."

Bridget has spent more than 1,500 days perched high above the trees working seasonally as a fire tower observer, tasked with spotting fires in Alberta. Along with teaching, these six-month contracts help to fund her ceramic projects, but they also mean that she generally ends up making work on her own and in many locations.

During the fire season, Bridget uses her seasonal studio in a shed next to the cabin where she lives when she is not up in the tower. The studio is equipped with a small kiln, wheel, glaze lab and woodshop. In order to watch for fires, Bridget must climb a 110-foot-tall tower to an eight-by-eight-foot octagon-shaped room that has no power or water. At times she will use a pulley system to haul clay up to the tower, or she will draw, but the majority of her ceramic work is done on the ground during her off-hours. She has also developed techniques that have enabled her to work anywhere with very little equipment, such as a preference for working on the floor (meaning she does not require large work tables) or designing objects with multiple smaller parts so that she can fire them separately in her small portable test kiln and then assemble them at a later date (making the transportation and firing of larger objects more manageable).

Depending on the project, when she is not stationed in northern Alberta watching for fires, Bridget rents studio space or participates in residencies. This flexibility enables her to seek out larger equipment and building facilities when required.

"I take pride in being able to make the most of a space," she states. "Over the years my studios have ranged from a basement hallway to a public, street-level-access exhibition and making space. I have also joined hacker/maker spaces, often allowing me to access 3D printers, laser cutters, computers, CNC mills and woodshops."

PATRICIA GRIFFIN

California potter Patricia Griffin is surrounded by nature, and much of her inspiration comes from the natural world. "I love being out in nature, and my home studio faces the sea in one direction and a wild preservation area in the other," she says. Through her bold, graphic line work and whimsical depictions of the natural world, Patricia brings nature to the table and home in a tactile way, with her mugs, bowls and vases covered in a myriad of images and motifs of the natural world, connecting the person who uses them to the world around them in a lighthearted and accessible way.

Patricia came to ceramics after a long career in marketing and design, and was able to successfully draw on her experience to turn her passion into a business. "Clay and art saved me," she says. "I was a busy business owner with staff and a family counting on me—a mom, a 'do everything for everybody type A' person. I ended up in therapy 25 years ago trying to fix my unhappiness. The therapist asked me to get the book *The Artist's Way: A Spiritual Path to Higher Creativity* by Julia Cameron, and I agreed to follow that process, eventually ending up in a community college clay class (rushing to and from client meetings before and after class). It was crazy and exhilarating to find myself doing something so seemingly frivolous as making pottery. But my awareness expanded in ways I could not have anticipated. I made new friends who were not connected to my business world." Over the course of her ceramics career, she has attended community college courses and workshops across the United States, and finds online resources particularly helpful.

"Play and experimentation were what propelled me into ceramics—and has kept me going. Whenever I feel pressure from commission due dates, shows, etc., I make a studio play date with myself. Sometimes it's a future date, and that's okay. Just the idea will calm me down and give me something to look forward to."

After 13 years of operating a gallery with an attached "working studio," where visitors could shop and see her work, Patricia recently closed the brick-and-mortar gallery and established a studio at home while simultaneously increasing her gallery representation, online sales and number of workshops she conducts two or three times every quarter. Her home-based studio is located halfway between San Francisco and Los Angeles, in the small seaside village of Cambria. She throws using a stand-up wheel and trims her work on a regular sit-down wheel in a converted greenhouse in her garden, where she can hear the ocean. Wheel work is broken up with hand-building time so as to avoid overtaxing her body, and Patricia usually works in cycles of throwing and hand-building followed by surface decoration, bisque firing, glazing and a final firing.

When she closed her retail gallery and studio, she converted her garage into a hand-building and finishing studio with work tables, a slab roller, an extruder and two electric kilns, with a separate glazing area. Although she does do some underglazing and etching

in the garage, she says that "much of this work is done at our kitchen table in the evening." She has also been known to commandeer the driveway in the name of clay: "When it's time to reclaim and pug clay, I roll my pugger out to the driveway, where I can see and hear the ocean in-between pugging sessions, and when the job is done I can hose off the driveway for an easy clean."

In order to operate a successful ceramics-related business, Patricia says, there are a few things you need: "Dogged determination, grit and patience, combined with insatiable curiosity, marketing savvy and a willingness to embrace risk." To this day, she still relies on her marketing background and spends a part of each day researching and learning what new opportunities and marketing tools she can apply to her business. She finds that her biggest challenge in operating her own business is balancing her desire to freely create with the need to operate her studio as a business—but as she wisely asserts, "I recognize there would be no studio or business without getting my pots out there and sharing them."

Last year, Patricia became certified as a California Naturalist, and nature journaling became a part of her process: "It's less about making 'art' and more about noticing the beauty around me, but I do believe that what I notice has made its way into my ceramic pieces." Just like going out for a rejuvenating hike or spending some time outdoors, Patricia's nature-inspired work brings a sense of joy and of connection to the natural world. Her tactile mugs, bowls and vases are alive with nature-filled stories and imagery. ❋

"I love the idea that my work lives on in other people's homes and hands, that it serves a purpose. I'm inspired by the personal connections that I have with people who engage with it. Much of my work is commissioned to celebrate special days, friendships and events. It delights me to know that a piece I made is reminding someone of a special memory, place or favourite animal."

"My work wants to be considered, engaged with, touched."

patriciagriffinceramics.com
@patriciagriffinceramics

SURFACE DECORATION

Patricia is inspired by traditional woodcuts and transferware because of the innovative combination of pattern and imagery. The Internet is her never-ending source for imagery that is rich in pattern and narrative. In order to create her bold black-and-white woodcut-like designs, Patricia employs sgraffito and Mishima techniques, which are also core skills she teaches in her two-day workshops on mark-making. "Sgraffito" comes from the Italian word for "scratching." This technique, often undertaken during the leather-hard state, involves scratching, inscising or carving a design through a layer of slip to reveal the contrasting clay colour underneath, resulting in bold patterns, images and textures. Mishima—a Japanese term inspired by imported Korean wares—is also done during the leather-hard state and involves inlaying contrasting-coloured slip into incised lines. The excess slip is then removed with a rib or sanded away once the piece is dry, leaving intricate incised lines on the surface of the vessel. Patricia's favourite tool for her line work is from DiamondCore Tools and is "a ball-stylist with a very small, sharp tip. When my clay (smooth B-Mix from Laguna) is at just the right consistency, I use it to make ultra-thin, crisp lines."

A MEDITATIVE PRACTICE

VICKI GRIMA

"My work is informed by the intricacies of the natural world—weathered surfaces and forms, microscopic textures and patterns, and the evidence of the passing of time."

To some, the repetitive pinching of clay is a form of relaxation and escape that is just as meditative and soothing as the rhythmic lapping of ocean waves. This is the case for Vicki Grima, from Sydney, Australia, whose goal is to "make simple organic forms that echo ocean-worn shells, pebbles and coastal rocks. I use the making of my work to calm my mind, aiming for gentle curves and simplicity. Some of my work is decorated with intricately textured and/or patterned dots, and I enjoy losing myself in obsessive patterning of surfaces. This activity allows me to experience a type of meditation." In short, her process is full of considered, meditative moments and actions that are the foundation of her intimate objects. The smallest of details, such as the slight lip of her vessels or her repetitive pattern work on her brooches, point to the nuances of nature and to Vicki's close connection to it.

Vicki says that although she considers herself a self-taught ceramist, "throughout my life I have continuously sought out creative people, exposing myself to ideas, skills and the creativity of other makers. Through my own teaching, I have also learned a lot from my students." She made her first "things with clay" in secondary school and then received formal training in art education. In the 1980s and 1990s, she taught art to secondary students and adults, and then, through Teacher Training Australia, taught fellow educators who "shared her passion for integrating visual arts through the whole curriculum." In 2005, she started working for the Australian Ceramics Association and since then has balanced her time between her ceramic practice and working for the Association as executive officer and journal editor.

"Form, surface, technique and firing all come together in a successful work in a way in which no one aspect is dominant. There's a cohesiveness to the work. It's meant to be. If any one aspect dominates, I question the success of that work."

Vicki works on a small, intimate scale and balances her time between making and office work, and her studio reflects this. When required, her home studio can double as an office space. It is small, consisting of two tables, or "work benches," nestled up against window-covered walls that overlook her garden and the Sydney airport. The studio is also equipped with a sink and storage area for some of her favourite mark-making tools, such as shells, driftwood, rocks and pebbles. Additional storage and her front-loading 1982 three-and-a-half-cubic-foot electric kiln are located in her garage. Of her kiln, she states, "it has been perfect for me. I often think it is one of the reasons I am still making ceramics."

The coastal areas near Vicki's home studio serve as inspiration for her work. Photography is an important part of her practice—she rarely draws—and she takes a lot of photographs during her regular nature walks. She also photographs her finished pots in interesting or meaningful environments, such as the beach or a particular rock shelf, which then inspires future pieces when she looks back at her photography.

"I am inspired by the patterns and textures of nature, in particular those that occur as the result of the passing of time— pitted rock pools, growth lines on shells, surface patterns created by water and wind. I take photos rather than draw. I like simple stitching on textiles and engraved lines in an etching."

She begins most of her pinch pot work—bowls, scooped forms and brooches—with a small ball of clay. "I move my hands in a spiral movement—a meditative practice done often with my eyes closed to feel the thickness of the walls as they form," Vicki says. "I explore the feel of clay, its strength and its fragility. My bowl forms are made to nestle in the hand. I seek the beauty in handmade details—fingerprints, delicate edges and decoration that unravels as the viewer gets closer and then holds the pot." She rarely joins pieces of clay together, instead focusing—meditatively—on the expanding process of pinching: "I assess as I go, question every movement, every indent." Her process is slow and she pays special attention to the edges and rims of her forms, aiming for a strong but thin and flowing edge—a nod to the flowing forms found in ocean and coastal environments.

In addition to her vessels, Vicki has made brooches for over three decades. "I like that they are precious and personal; they can be worn, and are accessible

(price-wise) to most people," she says. She loves exploring the infinite possibilities with making multiples, she says, and enjoys every part of her process, from pinching the malleable clay to wood- and lustre-firing.

Vicki's work spans the functional, sculptural and decorative; it is designed to have a broad appeal and to nestle into the hand so that there is a connection between environment, vessel and user. Her pieces are contemplative, intimate and relate to the natural world, while also reflecting her process. "Each work leads on to the next work," she says. "But to see my finished work in use is the very best!" ✻

vickigrima.com.au
@vickigrima

IN THE STUDIO AND OFFICE

Since 2005, Vicki has worked as executive officer for the Australian Ceramics Association and as editor of the *Journal of Australian Ceramics*. As executive officer, she works with the Association's 1,350-plus members from across Australia. The journal, begun in 1962, is published three times a year and features everything from artist profiles to critical essays, to exhibition and book reviews, and information related to ceramics education and workshops. It is an important resource for ceramists, students, galleries and collectors. In addition to this work, Vicki is also director of the Australian Ceramics Triennale, a four-day international contemporary ceramics conference that brings together artists, educators and theorists from around the world. Needless to say, Vicki has a lot on her plate, but she also manages to squeeze some time for making into any remaining gaps in her busy schedule. Doing so, she says, provides her "with a place to ponder the beauty in handmade details." As she says, "There is no typical studio work week. I fit my studio work into any spare time I have when I feel like making. It may be a few hours after my evening meal, a full day on a weekend, or maybe 30 minutes grabbed between a dog walk and heading off to work in my day job." Her ceramics practice, she says, is sustainable because it has become a way for her to find a "calm place." She sells her work through a local outlet and group exhibitions.

FICTIVE FLORETS

JULIE MOON

Fashion in the 1970s is easily identifiable—whether it be the synthetic fabrics, bold and colourful patterns, oversized shirt collars, long handmade tunic-like tops or David Bowie's Tokyo Pop vinyl suit by Kansai Yamamoto. There is a feel and look to the decade. The same can be said for domestic interiors of the time, dominated by that particular avocado green colour, covered from floor to ceiling with patterned wallpaper and shag carpets, and filled with plants—you know it when you see it.

Julie Moon of Toronto, Ontario, describes herself as a child of the 1970s, born to Korean-immigrant parents, who since highschool has idealized and romanticized aspects of the 1960s and 1970s hippie culture. "I'm into the idea of a love-driven social structure, rejecting societal norms, fighting for racial and gender inequality," she says. "I've always associated inclusivity with the counterculture of that era. I could envision myself being there." Her current series of abstracted, fantastical botanical sculptures brings together her love of this particular moment in time and its graphic arts with her background in textile design. In it, she combines form and surface to explore how culture influences our relationship with nature. "My experiences in nature and with the natural world, from childhood to adulthood, have been very limited," she explains. "I mostly experience nature through culture, and this indirect relationship creates a sense of fiction and fantasy in how I view and understand it."

Before working with ceramics, Julie studied fashion at George Brown College in Toronto and worked for over a decade "learning the ins and outs of the garment industry." She continued her studies in

"Whether you're a hobbyist or a professional artist using ceramics, we come to understand how seductive and engaging the materials and processes can be. Putting your hands into clay and shaping it into something is what people have done all over the planet through the ages. It's something we can all intuit."

textile design in the fibre arts program at the Ontario College of Art and Design, and while in her fourth year took a ceramic hand-building class. "I instantly fell in love with the tactile and sensual properties of working with clay," she recalls. "The rest is history." She completed an MFA at New York State College of Ceramics at Alfred University and has participated in a number of residencies in the United States and Germany. Julie asserts that although her studies taught her how to generate ideas, problem solve and foster lasting friendships, making is the best way to learn about new techniques and materials: "The better part of my education has occurred in communal studios. To practice in environments where you're in constant contact with stellar work and in close proximity to experienced and driven artists is such an incredible way to learn and stay motivated."

Throughout her career, Julie has focused on using form as a canvas for surface design. Her botanical sculptures often begin with a quick, loosely rendered sketch of a plant species. She begins a piece by pinching a base and then building it up with coils: "I almost always build from bottom to top, but I like to keep my options open, stopping every once in a while to see if there's another direction to move towards. During the process, I often abandon the sketch and make changes." Whenever possible, Julie will dedicate an eight- to nine-hour studio day to building. She likes to work fast and finds her Bernzomatic high-intensity trigger torch to be particularly useful, as it allows her to firm up the clay as she builds. Once the form is complete, she attaches decorative elements to the surface and then bisque fires the work in one of her three electric kilns.

After the bisque firing, she will often let the work "hang out" in the studio for a while until she commits to a surface design. Her first step when glazing is to sketch out the design in pencil, directly on the bisqued form. Then she "colours" in her design with products

such as Mayco Stroke and Coat glazes, as she appreciates the colour range, convenience and wide firing range of these commercial products. For Julie, glazing requires greater concentration and organization than building. "It can be hard to look that closely at something for long periods," she says. "I often need to break up glazing over a few days, spending three to four hours at a time." During this phase, she often stops partway through and low-fires the work in order to get a better sense of what she has done.

With her Still Life and her Acid Garden series, in which her fantastical floral shapes and arrangements create a fictitious otherworldly garden within the gallery, Julie takes familiar motifs associated with plants and processes them through her own heavily mediated experiences of nature. Julie explains that most of her experiences with nature have been filtered through a mix of 1960s and 1970s material and visual culture and design. She has great appreciation for graphic and textile arts, and avidly follows many illustrators and comic book artists. Some of her favourite designers are Sonia Delaunay, Raoul Dufy and Nathalie du Pasquier, she says, noting their ability to move effortlessly between mediums. "It seems almost magical to me how illustrators are able to invent entire worlds in their own unique voice. This admiration likely comes from my own aspiration to create an original and varied body of work that also feels authentic and connected." With all of this cultural inspiration, Julie's flowers and plants distort and take on new shapes and meanings, resulting in vibrant, energetic, highly decorated plant forms that have a graphic and flattened sensibility. Sometimes, as in the case of Julie's fictive florets, paging through history and appreciating design can be just as inspiring as a walk in the wilderness. ❋

"Aside from pieces in my wholesale production, I tend to never make things more than once. Variation becomes a way for me to play and try new things. Also, when things go wrong, problem solving becomes an opportunity to get creative or unconventional."

"In an increasingly digital world, the tangible and tactile qualities of ceramics are appealing, not just for consumers but also through the experience of making."

CERAMICS FOR THE BODY

juliemoon.com
@juliemoooon

Since completing graduate studies in 2010, Julie has maintained a full-time studio practice. She explains that while she loves working for herself and setting her own schedule, it can be stressful: "I get nervous about my finances and have a hard time turning down paying jobs. I find that I'm often shifting priorities in order to make money and pay those bills!" In order to do this, Julie has "cultivated" a multifaceted practice that involves participating in craft sales and art exhibitions, collaborating with other companies to develop decorative home objects and custom art pieces for hotel interiors, conducting hand-building classes and workshops in her studio, and designing and creating a wholesale collection of wearable ceramics in addition to her other bodies of work. In fact, after finishing grad school, she relied almost exclusively on the sales of her jewellery, which she had initially started to make as an undergraduate. Her interest in fashion and design is particularly evident in the bold geometric aesthetic of her jewellery, but her ceramic knowledge comes through with her choice of durable high-fire clay bodies. She finds designing smaller-scale work enjoyable, as it allows her to explore different techniques, materials and glaze combinations. She sells her ceramic jewellery through Etsy and various shops and galleries across North America but keeps the business small, making everything herself. Since taking on more teaching, Julie has been able to slow down her jewellery production: "The precision and repetition required to make this work has been especially hard on my hands," she says. "I'm trying to be kinder to myself and pay attention to the preservation of this ageing body! The way that the jewellery is made now, doesn't seem sustainable long-term. Change is inevitable and it's important to adapt."

IMPRESSED NATURE

SARAH PIKE

As far back as Sarah Pike can remember she has loved clay and the act of making things. When she was five years old, she made a "leggy little frog" in a city-run class, and by the time she was 13, she had bought a used Skutt kiln with her savings. Her dad constructed a little room for her in the basement of their house, and that is where she remembers fashioning small things out of coils and slabs.

"When I say I bought a kiln as a young teenager, you might misunderstand me," Sarah is quick to clarify. "I didn't buy the kiln and say 'I will be a potter.' I simply loved making things and a kiln was the tool I needed at the time. I came from a family of makers; project people. In our home, there were always multiple things on the go: boat building, renos, stained glass, basket weaving, macramé, soapstone carving, painting and drawing. It was just normal to make things. I liked clay, so I bought a kiln." Today, Sarah, a self-professed "outdoors gal," is a full-time functional potter located in Fernie, British Columbia. She is best known for her hand-built textured slab wares, which feature, among other things, strong, stamped pattern work and minimalist, rustic renderings of nature in the form of trees, branches and leaves.

Sarah's home studio, located right next to a beaver pond in the Rocky Mountains, is a long shed-roofed garage with windows down one side. The studio has heated concrete floors that are warm in the winter and cool in the summer. It is equipped with two electric kilns, a pug mill, one small table and two large, sturdy tables. The smallest table was built by Sarah and her father when she was around seven years old, and it "started a life-long connection of making things

"I still remember the first time I drank out of a mug I made. It was magic. No, not the mug—the mug was *not* magic. It was a heavy, lumpy little thing. I'm talking about the act of making something out of a squishy, messy material, firing it and then using it—the process and the function all tied up in this beautiful, sensual experience. I was hooked."

"I hope that my absolute love and awe of the natural landscape is evident in my pots."

together." The two larger tables are her favourite tools, as she uses them for hand-rolling her clay slabs. Her father built the first table for her around 15 years ago: "He used clear fir, mortise and tenon joints, no holds barred. A solid work table is pure joy to work on. Making pots on the worktables he built for me is a beautiful circle." Sarah's father helped lay the foundation of working with your hands all those years ago. "Now I make a living making pots on the tables he built for me. A couple of years ago, we built the second table together—these two beauties truly are my favourite tools."

After studying ceramics at the Alberta College of Art and Design in Calgary, the University of Colorado in Boulder and the University of Minnesota in Minneapolis, Sarah thought she would continue exploring atmospheric firings, but eventually realized that building an atmospheric kiln was not in her foreseeable future. Instead, through harnessing the "adaptability" required of any business owner, she developed surfaces that replicated what she liked in salt-

or soda-fired work. Dissatisfaction with the raw areas on her pots led her to use red clay—she found it more pleasing, and especially liked how it broke through the glaze to emphasize textures and seams. Although she can't quite remember when she first started making stamps for clay, she asserts that her obsession with stamping started when she switched to slab building: "A freshly rolled slab of soft clay is an ideal canvas for pushing texture into, because the smooth table under the slab acts as counter pressure, leaving a sharp and even impression in the clay," Sarah explains. Constructing her pots out of slabs takes a lot of time but it creates an ideal surface for the texturing and stamping that Sarah is known for today.

Sarah finds inspiration for her work from the natural world, minimalist interior design, ceramic history, textiles, textured metals, antique tinware forms, prairie farm architecture and still-life paintings. She uses her camera, especially when she is out in the garden, woods and mountains, to capture things that inspire her. She also snaps photos of patterns on

people's clothes, tiles or pressed metal ceilings. She does not draw as much as she used to, she says, but still sketches quick ideas. When developing a new form, she often works out the design through a series of maquettes. "These are quick, three-dimensional sketches that I can tweak and play with until I get a design I want to explore further," she says. "When I'm satisfied with the rough form, I move to larger slabs and play with dimensions and proportions. At this point, I will usually fire a few of the new designs to completion so I can test out functionality. More tweaks are often required. Sometimes these tweaks are obvious. Sometimes the pot will sit on a shelf in my periphery until I figure out how to tackle it again."

Although her tendency is to get lost in the cycle of making, she heads outdoors for exercise and a mental refresh: "Filling my lungs and heart and head with fresh air." She might take some photographs. "Then I bring all this back to the studio." Sarah says that although no one chooses the life of a craftsperson to get rich, "ideally we can make a living within this lifestyle.

My goal is to not compromise quality for quantity, to allow time for my work to evolve, even if it is in the tiniest little increments, and to make connections with my customers and fellow craft folk."

Sarah recently had to face heartache and physical pain that made her feel numb to creativity. "I have had a tough couple of years of grief and injury that have forced me to take a deeper look at why I am in this and where I want to be," she says. "We get lost in the grind of daily making and suddenly months have passed. It is not always easy to make space for bursts of growth and experimentation." In order to trigger new growth and reclaim a creative frame of mind, she challenged herself to make a new stamp or texture tool every day for 30 days. She recalls, "Even when my heart was heavy and I felt I had nothing left to give, my self-inflicted challenge forced me into the studio every day, and slowly I felt that familiar yet lost electrical buzz. Using social media added accountability to the challenge, but also helped me to re-engage with our community." ❋

"I'm not a huge fan of the word 'failure,' because it implies finality: I tried something, it didn't work, game over. The whole process of making is wrapped up in trying, pushing boundaries, experimenting, questioning. There is no such thing as failing in research. Of course, things don't always turn out how I planned, but that is just part of the process. I recently took a surf lesson and the instructor said you should only be successfully surfing 10% of the waves you attempt to surf. If you are surfing them all, you aren't pushing yourself. I like that. It embraces the tumbles and the misses as learning opportunities."

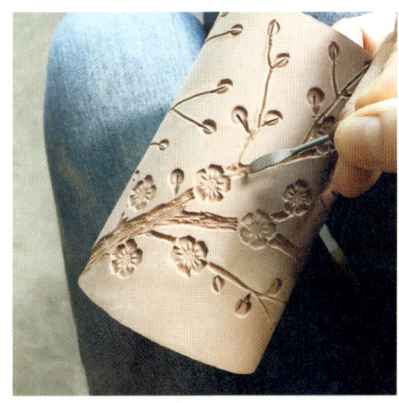

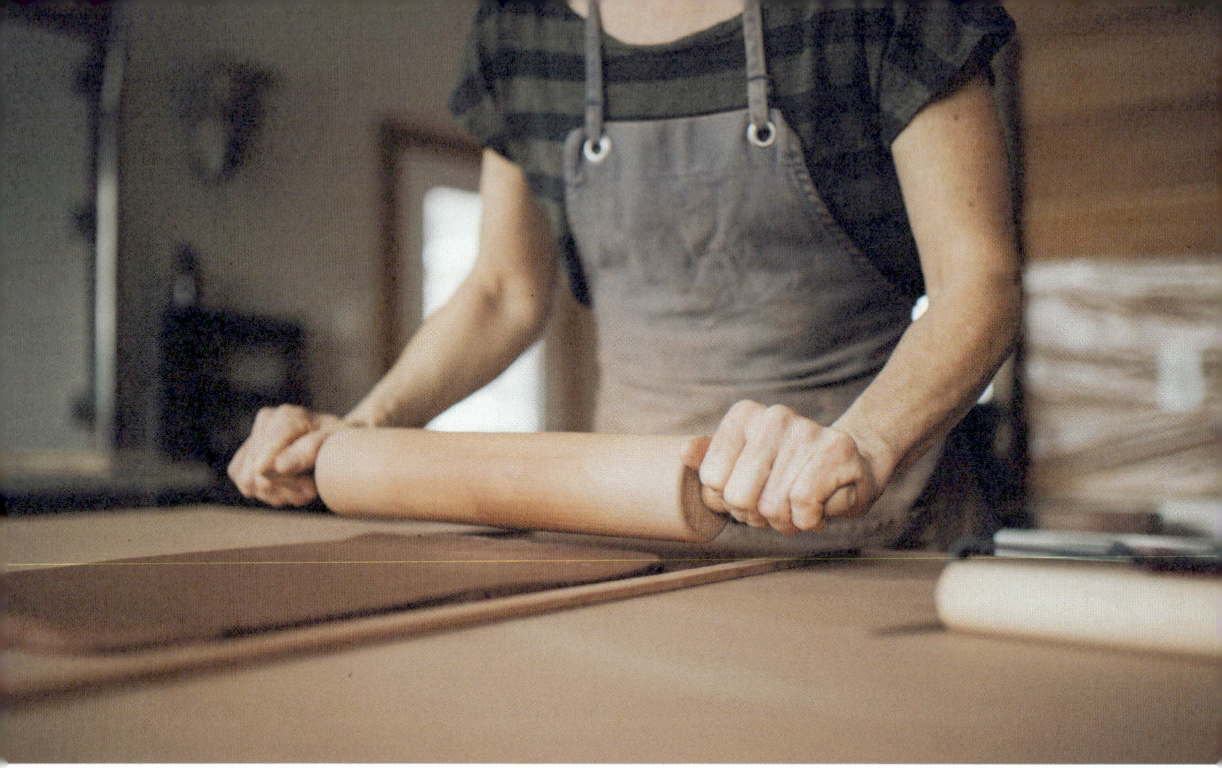

HAND CARVED BISQUED STAMPS

Sarah's surface decoration relies heavily on texture: "I'm a huge fan of how something feels to the sense of touch. Texture can be beautiful in a visual and tactile way—perfect for functional objects intended for use." She textures her work with a variety of custom-made stamps and stamp rollers, which allow her to add decoration to her work at the "raw stage of making." At this early stage, she can distort and change the patterns by stretching the clay, something she really enjoys doing. For Sarah, texture also simplifies glazing, as her pots are simply dunked in glaze and are then ready for the kiln.

She explains that, for her, the key to making stamps is "to embrace your inner fastidious, meticulous, overly precise self, then get super obsessed." She begins by cutting the basic shape for a new stamp out of a slab of clay, which she then sets aside to firm up to the leather-hard state. At that point, the blank stamp is ready for carving—keeping in mind, she says, that incised lines on the stamp will be raised on the final piece. Obsession comes into play once the clay starts to dry, as it is important to clean up any burrs and to "tweak" and define the details over and over again. The final step, once the stamp is almost dry, is to create a test imprint by carefully pressing the new stamp into wet clay. If Sarah is satisfied with the outcome, she will bisque the stamp so that it will easily pull away from the clay when it is used. If she does not like what she sees with the test, she will either refine it some more or recycle it into the reclaim bucket.

sarahpikepottery.com
@sarahpikepottery

A WONDROUS MICRO VIEW

SARAH RAYNER

Sarah Rayner grew up with clay, as both her mother and brother are potters. She has fond memories of sitting up until all hours of the night beside a wood kiln, watching and waiting. But, as she recalls, "I didn't enjoy using clay at all! The texture and feel of wet, gritty clay on my hands were not at all pleasurable." In the late 1990s, Sarah majored in textiles at the University of Southern Queensland in Toowoomba, Australia, and after practicing art for over 30 years, turned to clay about six years ago. Her friend and fellow Australian ceramist Shannon Garson introduced her to porcelain "as a means to create sculptural works, which I had been experimenting with in both textiles and plaster. Despite my initial resistance, I was completely seduced by the nature of this material."

"Humans' desire to learn more about our natural world, to have and to hold it, to own and control it, is proving to be detrimental to the healthy existence of the planet. I spend many hours contemplating and musing about this and storing my wonder and despair inside these tiny objects. I hope they inspire people to look closely, to appreciate and to respect the sheer wonder and importance of the natural world around them."

Today, Sarah lives and works in Wootha, Australia, on a 50-acre bush block surrounded by flora and fauna. "I closely identify with my immediate environment and feel incredibly lucky to live where I do and to have the opportunity to closely observe plants, insects, birds and animals in their ongoing cycle of reproduction and survival," Sarah says. "It's a truly humbling experience." This close, intimate proximity to nature is apparent in Sarah's work, in her intricate porcelain sculptures of plant gynoecium (the female part of the plant that develops into the fruit and seeds), which, through a micro–macro sense of scale, bring with them a sense of wonder.

Literary historian Stephen Greenblatt describes wonder as the power of an object to stop a viewer in their tracks, sweeping them into a state of "enchanted looking" in which everything else around the object is excluded. Wonder can foster "resonance," which involves a desire to learn more and feel more, which in turn expands one's world. Sarah's porcelain sculptures, which are underpinned by her interest in

museology and informed by her natural environment, do exactly that. "The work requires the viewer to look closely in order to fully realize the hidden details: crevices, pinholes, interior cavities filled with flowers and seeds," she explains. "The scale and expectation that the viewer needs to make close inspection create an intimacy between the audience and the work. Whilst the sculptures are informed by seedpods and the inside structures of plants, they are interpretative, so they morph and change from the original inspiration, becoming familiar yet strange objects. This creates a sense of wonder and questioning from the viewer."

You can't help but get lost in the tiniest of porcelain folds or in the rhythmic staccato of hundreds of pinholes, but the micro details in Sarah's work have a wondrous macro effect as well: seeds, flowers, pods and pistils never looked so beautiful or complex. After seeing her sculptures, it becomes hard not to notice these objects in day-to-day life. Subsequently, the world becomes a much bigger place.

"My interest lies in the tiny and seemingly insignificant details of the forest—a micro view of seedpods and flowers, which leads to a fascinating world of intricate and complex things, the understated and overlooked in hidden spaces and places," Sarah says. "I like to scrutinize and dissect these amazing little structures, examining the form, textures, cracks and crevices, and the way layers peel back to reveal sensuous interiors, which cradle precious seeds." Her process involves ample bushwalking in order to observe and collect. On her walks, she pays close attention to the metamorphosis of flower to seedpod. She collects samples of pods and plant material and then draws the relationships that she observes between them.

Sarah, who is represented by Gallery Sally Dan-Cuthbert, creates work for public art galleries and private homes. She begins her sculptural work by forming a basic shape in porcelain, then letting it firm up to a leather-hard state so that she can carve into it to refine the form and make it come alive. As Sarah is still not a fan of working with wet clay, this carving stage is particularly satisfying to her. Once the form is complete, she adds details and pinholes. "My work is slow, contemplative and meticulous in its construction," she explains. "The pieces are small and intimate, held and shaped within the curves of my hands and fingers." When the detail work is complete, the piece is dried, covered in terra sigillata and fired once. Terra sigillata—Italian for "sealed earth"—is a refined slip that can produce a soft sheen to a glossy surface. "The satin, white terra sigillata surface highlights the tiny pinholes and other textural details covering the outside of my pieces," Sarah says. "The finish is quiet, calm, sensuous and soft. The simplicity of the finish accentuates the form and the delicacy of my subject matter, and the beauty and vulnerability of all living things."

"I thrive on the process of making, the satisfaction of creating with my hands, the excitement of sharing this with others. Having the opportunity, space and time to make is an incredible privilege. This keeps me inspired and motivated."

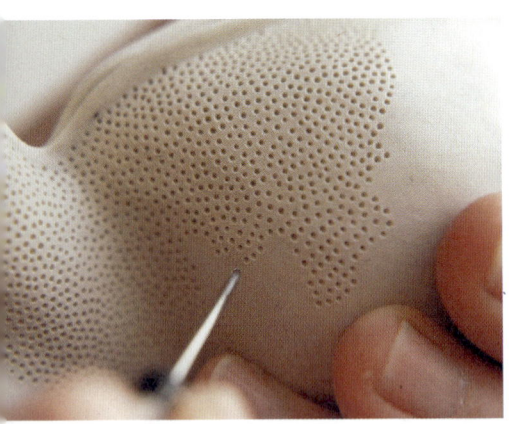

There is an underlying curiosity to Sarah's work around how things fit together in a natural and historical context and within contemporary society. "I'm compelled to make," Sarah says of her practice. "It keeps me grounded and happy. It's a source of meditation and contemplation, with many layers of musing stored inside the little objects I make; it becomes a way of processing the world around me. Combining my love of the natural environment and satisfying my curiosity through exploration and observation and art-making is a joy." Her sculptures, which reflect her sense of joy, are also wondrous objects that relate to the mysteries of nature. ✱

"My particular interest lies in the reproductive organs and life cycles of plants, and the symbiotic relationships they have with insects and birds, which is an incredibly delicate balance."

"The cyclic nature and metamorphic growth patterns of these miniscule forms is a source of wonderment and joy."

A COCOON OF INSPIRATION

Sarah's studio is located in a small open room within the home she shares with her husband, Jeff, on the Sunshine Coast Hinterland in Queensland, Australia. "I don't separate the studio from home life; it's very much a part of it," she says. Their home is filled with collections and objects such as haberdashery items, vintage fabrics, bones, artworks and other objects of interest, which Sarah credits as having a huge influence on her artistic practice. "I arrange our collection continually, changing pieces around and playing with their relationship to one another, creating new dialogues."

The couple run a small business in natural area management and strive to live as sustainably as possible: their house is completely solar powered, they collect their own water in storage tanks and they have a large vegetable patch and fruit trees. In addition, Sarah's electric kiln is located at a friend's solar-powered house. Her studio overlooks the bushland that surrounds their home, meaning all Sarah can hear is "birdsong, cicadas and the breeze through the trees." Like the rest of her house, Sarah's studio is designed to cocoon her with inspiration: jars of dried organic matter sit atop her desk, test tubes filled with seeds line her shelves, books on plants are nestled here and there, old botanical postcards are tacked to her board, two 1940s mannequin heads peer down from above, a collection of aluminum shoe lasts hang irregularly from a bottom shelf and her desk is always covered in native flowers and seed pods from the garden or surrounding bushland. The space is cozy, sustainable and inspirational.

sarahrayner.com.au
@sarah.rayner

NAOMI CLEMENT

LIFE/WORK BALANCE

WRITTEN BY CAROLE EPP

THE PAINTER AS POTTER

HEATHER DAHL

"When I graduated from art school I imagined a career path that pursued getting grants, artist residencies, grad school, galleries and teaching at a postsecondary level. At some point after having kids my definition of success was that I wanted to make a living as an artist to support my family and to allow me to make work as a full-time artist."

From a studio just steps outside her home in rural British Columbia to the hectic bustle of a studio in a co-op in Vancouver, Heather Dahl has the best of both worlds in her ceramic practice. She has time alone to focus and develop work in solitude as well as access to the energy of community studio interactions with other artists and face-to-face time with clients. "Most of my wet-work is done at home, where I can keep tabs on the drying temperature of the pots," Heather says. "I have a home office and try to take my photos at home, so some days are computer days more than making-pot days. I commute an hour to my Vancouver studio two to three days a week to mix glazes or slips, to glaze, fire, slip-cast, meet with clients or drop off work at my local stores."

These relationships with shops and retailers have been the backbone of Heather's Dahlhaus Studio since 2008. "When my kids were three and five, I took a self-employment program to help kick-start my studio practice," she explains. "I realized I had nothing to lose by following a long-standing dream of mine." That dream stretches back to her teen years, when she would visit the local pottery studios in the Fraser Valley. What appealed to Heather was the smell of the clay, its physicality, and the romantic infrastructure of brick gas kilns and studio spaces. Potters have a unique lifestyle and rhythm to their lives that tends to draw in the next generation of makers. Heather began her journey in clay with community classes that eventually lead to a BFA in ceramics and painting.

Heather's background education in painting continues to influence her ceramic work. The surface of the clay object is a focus in her practice. That is not

to say she disregards the form of the object, but rather that the surface is where her aesthetics and design references come to life. Occasionally we see her paintings on her Instagram feed or at open studios, perfectly matched aesthetically to her pottery. What pottery can offer that painting cannot, however, is what Heather describes as a "level of intimacy." Heather is inspired by the rituals of object use. How one holds a cup or dish is actually dictated by its design and production, and all the considerations that an artist laboriously puts into the work. That relationship between the maker and the user of the object is ever-present.

LOOKING BACK AND TRENDING FORWARD

Heather's work is mid-century modern design coupled with a contemporary influence. Her colour selections are very much on-trend, but there are underlying nods to and nostalgia for the straightforward simplicity that is characteristic of Bauhaus design. Heather has long been fascinated with the Bauhaus and the Arts and Crafts movement, starting her personal collection with a Danish teak desk at the age of 16. "I studied the Bauhaus and the Arts and Crafts movement in school and have been a thrift shopper and collector since I was young," she says. "I'm most interested in making work with an emphasis on well-crafted, simple forms paired with graphic/modern decoration. I love the process of working in clay, and different printmaking, painting, paper-cutting and folk art traditions have influenced my work."

"I'm drawn to colour combinations and patterns, so sometimes my sketchbook is a way for me to pull out one element of a pattern I like or a combination of shapes that I'm drawn to. For my screen-printed monoprints or glaze inlay work, I'll sit down with black tape or paper and start mapping out patterns just by cut and paste. These get scanned into the computer and printed off, or reassembled in Photoshop before becoming screenprints."

MAKING NEW THINGS

Having a family means that it is difficult for Heather to get away for residencies or to have time to make new work. "I've found ways of inserting opportunities for me to develop those ideas or ways of making into my regular routine," she explains. "I have at times blocked off a month as my 'in-studio residency' to break out of my routine." Lacking her own soda firing kiln, she took a class so she could use new clay, glazes and decorating process. "My work is always evolving in the midst of sustaining the studio with work that I've become known for. I think of success as being able to be free to make creative decisions in the work that I'm making. I have always been interested in evolving as a maker, which means my professional goals are often changing to suit the work I'm interested in making." ✣

dahlhausart.com
@dahlhausart

NAVIGATING THE MARKET

Heather's career trajectory has been balanced between artistic exploration and the demands of wholesale customers and clients. "The level of consistency I need to make the work desired by retailers has in some ways held back other parts of my career as an artist," she says. "The lack of reliable galleries has kept my work in the retail sector as well. So there's a tension between growing my career and creating a marketable product that sells well on the shelves of any home decor shop."

Heather believes that for her business to succeed she must be the one in control, navigating marketing and career trajectories. To be pushed and pulled, or have to rely on galleries, curators, write-ups in magazines or exhibitions is a tough path to follow. Artists can lose themselves while trying to live up to others' expectations or to the quick turnover of trends. For Heather, the freedom to straddle both design and craft in the ways that creatively fulfil and excite her, keeps her work sustainable.

"I am able to support myself, but it's been a really hard business to scale in Vancouver. The cost of rent for both my studio and housing is so high, and hiring assistants to help with volume orders makes the profit margins very tight."

LOVE LETTERS TO LIFE

NAOMI CLEMENT

As a self-declared pottery nomad, Naomi Clement has spent much of her career on the road, moving from one opportunity to the next, adding residencies and teaching gigs to her resume, and working alongside international ceramic artists. This year is different. She has bought her first home in Stratford, Ontario, where she is now in the process of setting up a studio in her basement. For the first time in a long time, Naomi is shifting gears to work in the quiet isolation of her home studio. Now she doesn't have to leave the house or change out of pyjamas when working. The effect this change in lifestyle will have on her work/life balance will be an interesting new adventure.

One of the best things about her new home? She finally gets to unpack her personal ceramic collection. Mementos from travels, friends and influential artists can now be part of her domestic environment in the same way that she wishes her pottery exists for others in their everyday life. In her teaching and travels, Naomi expounds on the value and necessity of handmade pottery. "I am a potter because I fundamentally believe that functional pots are a powerful vehicle for conveying ideas and creating change," she says. "Maybe they don't change the world with a thunderclap or a lightning bolt, but rather I believe that pots change us and our days through our interactions with them."

The home, family history and domestic life are themes that run deep in Naomi's work. "I use text elements taken from old family correspondence and ephemera to explore my family history and connect past and present," she explains. "Letters are digitally scanned, enlarged and then laser cut into newsprint.

"A quote that I go back to often is, 'the only thing harder than being an artist is not being an artist.' I'm not sure who said that, but it is pretty darn true. I tried not being an artist for years, but it didn't work so well. So, I remind myself of that when things get tough."

These newsprint text elements are then used in my decorative process, acting both as a stamp and resist for colour and texture." At first glance what appear as gestural lines of colour on her pots are actually those scanned letters. The script that once wove words from one person to another now exists as bold strokes of colour on her wares. "Handwriting is such a personal way of connecting, leaving your mark and telling your story—through this intimate process, we connect our thoughts to the physical world. Using the labour of my hands, I unite these traces of my past with functional objects that celebrate the tangible joy of the everyday."

COLOUR AS EMOTION

Naomi is also inspired by artistic sources such as Mark Rothko and Helen Frankenthaler: abstract painters who are known for their use of colour to convey emotions. Naomi's concise and deliberate use of colour draws out emotion and evokes nostalgia, and compels the eye to further investigate the surfaces of her pottery. Her choice of bold colours like red and orange sit in stark contrast to the distinct dark clay body that she is drawn to. Naomi uses this clay not just as a background canvas but as a collaborator in the final design. "Visually it provides a counterpoint to the colours and activity elsewhere on the pot," she says. "Leaving large sections of clay bare and unglazed, polished smooth to give a sense of comfort and of a life lived, provides a distinct physical contrast from the glossy surface of the glazed areas."

"We are living in an incredible time for ceramics. We have ready access to materials and methods and new technologies in an unprecedented way. Pair this with an ability to promote our own work to a wider audience through social media and other online platforms, and you get the rich and diverse ceramic field we are living in. Ceramics is also becoming more mainstream. In an overwhelmingly digital world, folks are increasingly looking for tangible, physical connections. Clay provides that."

"I believe that function is all about noticing: noticing the material, noticing the process and noticing the user. In our digital age, I believe there is a weight to this—seeing and acknowledging are powerful acts."

"My pots ask to be noticed and examined. I want them to convey a sense of a life lived, and a life still to be lived; they are about making connections and wanting to make connections. A snapshot of the journey, each pot is a tether that connects me to me, and me to you: a memory bound in mud-made-stone for years to come."

WHERE TO FIND JOY

Naomi's ceramic process is labour intensive, and thus the work commands a higher price point to be sustainable, but she does not shy away from that or attempt to find new methods to simplify her work. She sees herself as "a maker of things, rather than a doer of things." It is in the labour, the making, the repetition and the exploration that she finds joy. "As a material, clay is full of contradictions," she explains. "It is at once soft and hard, flexible and fragile, ephemeral and eternal. Like most artists who work with clay, I both love and hate the way it constantly challenges me as a maker and thinker."

Work/life balance is a challenge for most artists, even those who have the means to outsource some of the workload. Studio time versus business administrative time also demands a balance. No artist gets to be in the studio full time. "From daily production in the studio to writing grants, communicating with galleries, and promoting and selling my work directly, making a living as an artist requires perseverance, ingenuity and grit."

Naomi assesses which professional relationships and opportunities will add the most value relative to her labour output, including being selective about her relationships with galleries. Selling work directly to customers is more financially sustainable for an artist, but requires more time spent in marketing, packaging and shipping. One of Naomi's main galleries, Companion Gallery in Tennessee, is run by another ceramic artist, Eric Botbyl, and his wife, Jill. The understanding and sensibility that makers who are also gallery owners can bring to the gallery experience goes a long way in educating clients and customers. ✣

naomiclement.com
@naomikclement

THE CREATIVE PROCESS

"I'm not much of a sketcher, so I really work through ideas by making," says Naomi. Sometimes new work evolves slowly, through small tweaks and experimentation. Over time, this slow change and continual questioning build on each other, leading to end results that are quite different from where she started. "Other times, I'll have a specific form or idea in mind and attack the problem head-on, trying things out in the studio and creating new templates and moulds to achieve the desired result."

Various points of the process have their appeal, but for Naomi, the leather-hard stage is when she says she "falls in love with the work. It's when the pots feel most dear to me and most alive. There is a moment, usually just after I have finished decorating the pots, when I can still see them for all that they have been, and all that they might be. I like the finished objects that I make, but the reality is that they are placeholders for the pots that exist in my memory."

"I'm always thinking about the finished object from before I even start a piece. When the pot is still a lump of clay, I'm already thinking about how it will be glazed or finished. This thinking ahead allows me to create work that is hopefully cohesive and that feels balanced, and where the surface and form are integrated."

CLAY, WOOD AND FIRE

ROBIN DUPONT

It feels like a slogan of sorts—the mountains are calling—and for artist Robin Dupont it was a call that he couldn't resist. "I grew up in a city with a view of the Rocky Mountains," recalls Robin. "As soon as I was old enough I moved to them. Art school brought me back to the city, where I found the medium of clay. Upon finishing my education I ended up back in the mountains. My life of clay and living in the mountains has transformed my life, and shaped my career and who I am."

For the last 15 years, Robin and his family have called an acreage in the Slocan Valley just outside of Nelson, British Columbia, their studio, home and gallery. There, stunning landscapes act as a source of inspiration, and the amount of physical space allows Robin a lifestyle and studio set-up that fosters his creation of one-of-a-kind wood- and soda-fired pottery. The studio is situated in the walkout daylight basement of their home, but it pales in comparison to the wood-firing kiln shed, which is three times the size of the studio. The large size is required, explains Robin, "in order to accommodate drying wood in our moist climate—it's an inland temperate rain forest." These kilns are the beating heart of the process that is synonymous with Robin's work.

Like many artists in ceramics, Robin came to clay while studying other artistic disciplines, such as painting and sculpture; the material's versatility, however, won him over. "Clay can be used in so many different ways," Robin says: "architectural, culinary, spiritual, plumbing—and the medium has been used historically to inform and enhance our lives as a species." Material process, aesthetics and challenging preconceptions of functional ceramics are all central to his work.

"I am a maker. I love the process of interacting with materials and process. Whether I am making bread, coffee or pottery, or building kilns, I feel most at home when I am involved in the dialogue that happens with making and thinking critically about that interaction and what I produce."

Robin completed an MFA in ceramics, but his education also consists of informal training, work-studies, apprenticeships and residencies. "Through this period of education and networking, many people and institutions took me up on my offer to help in exchange for learning," he says. "I now run my own studio with this philosophy, and every year I have new people coming through the studio, learning about the process." He also brings this experience into his classroom at Kootenay Studio Arts at Selkirk College, in the hopes of highlighting the multitude of pathways to becoming an artist.

Robin is now at a stage in his career in which he can take on assistants and apprentices, and he often takes a community-based approach to the firing of his work. Firing wood and soda kilns are laborious processes—long days and nights of firings made manageable through collaboration and the support of other artists.

THE LANGUAGE OF THE LAND

Living and working on a mountainside acreage, Robin draws from the language and geologic history of the land, as a part of the aesthetics of his work. "I like to see evidence of the character of the clay," he says. "There is an aesthetic relationship to nature, landscape, geology, sometimes cosmos and astrology. I feel like so much of my output is determined by learning and the materials and processes. Much of this revolves around the atmospheric process. There is quite a range of surfaces that can be obtained in an atmospheric kiln. I look for deep, rich, layered surfaces, effects that reference a passage of time. Natural processes such as geology do this, creating marks of process that can inform or tell a story or narrative. My aesthetic is a balance of this intentional mark-making, but also the chaos of firing atmospherically. It is both random and contrived."

GALLERY ON WHEELS

Robin says he lives and breathes clay. Indeed, there is little separation between life and work intertwined on that acreage up in the mountains. Robin makes his living through ceramics, managing a balance of sales, workshops and teaching, but this wasn't always the case. "Skills that I have found helpful that I never dreamed I would have needed to be a potter are public speaking, graphic design, photography, masonry (for kiln building), electrical knowledge (for electric kiln maintenance) and backing up a trailer."

In 2015, Robin bought a 1959 Airstream that now functions on the property as a gallery space. The Airstream also travels as FORM mobile gallery, a portable gallery space for Robin to curate the work of other artists and bring their art to events such as clay conferences in different regions. Robin sees this project as an educational tool that sidesteps traditional gallery models; he can use it to reach new audiences for clay in unexpected venues. The Airstream gallery allows him to control how he sells his own work in a way that is not limited by commercial gallery obligations and expectations. That's not to say you can't find Robin's work in galleries, but as he says, "I only sell my work with galleries who foster a clientele that expects creative growth. I am not the kind of potter that you will build a matching set of dinnerware from over the course of a decade. The aesthetic of atmospheric firing is a direct record of the firing process and therefore it is helpful if this is communicated to the audience. It has been important for me to find galleries that will do this and take on this educational role." ❉

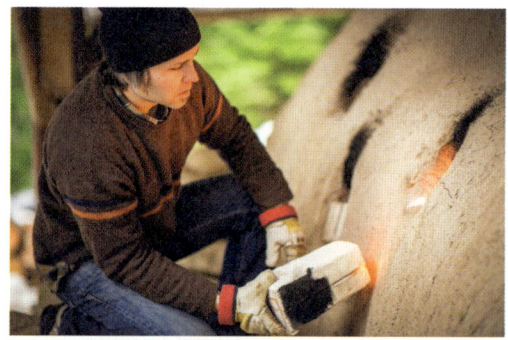

WOOD AND SODA FIRING

"For at least a few thousand years, wood was the principal fuel for firing pottery," explains Robin. "At some point in history, potters discovered that the wood ash would melt and affect the clay to produce subtle and beautiful surfaces on the work during the firing process. During a wood firing, the wood itself becomes the glaze—and at extremely high temperatures molten ash can run, drip and layer the pots with this ash glaze." Contemporary ceramic enthusiasts still pursue this tradition. "They go to great lengths to collect, chop and stack the wood so that they can stoke the kiln for many continuous hours per days to orchestrate these unique surfaces."

Because Robin's kilns are so large, he has to make work for at least two weeks—and often a month or two—before firing. "I always find that the most growth and ideas come the longer I'm working on that making cycle. Creativity builds and everything starts to flow and is less effort. Because of this I am always trying to extend the making and push the firing back. It's not that I don't enjoy the firing, in fact every time I fire I just want to load up the kiln and fire again, so often I shape my work cycles around this."

Soda firing is an atmospheric firing process that makes use of sodium. "Similar to with wood firing, bisqued pots are loaded into the kiln without any pre-applied glaze," Robin explains. "When sodium bicarbonate is tossed into the kiln near top temperature, the soda instantly vaporizes and is carried by the flame throughout the chamber. The soda

"One of my mentors once said: don't look at the pots that I make for inspiration, look at the pots I look at for inspiration."

acts as a glaze and reacts chemically with the forms to create a surface on the pots."

Robin's work is very much about surface-form relationships, and over the years he has developed his forms in response to certain characteristics of surface he can obtain with firing in a particular way. "The wood kiln is an interesting case because of the variety of surfaces available," he notes. "I may get something crusty out of the side stoke area and something slick, clean and refined out of the back. Then, of course, there is everything in between. Because clay is so malleable it allows for the record of the most subtle of nuances, and those nuances are a narrative of sorts, a layer of meaning and information to be communicated to your audience."

In these firing processes, there are so many variables at play that one has to balance expectations with reality. "Through the process of collecting, chopping and stacking of wood, making of the work, loading of the work and then the five-day firing, the expectations build for how good the work that comes out of the kiln will be," Robin says. "Expectations are rarely met because it's impossible to look and assess objectively after a firing, after all the labour and time, even after a solid night's sleep. The truth is, the surfaces are often so sophisticated that you can't recognize or have the ability to assess them objectively at first. Regardless of how good or bad the firings end up, I learn as much, if not more, from the failures as I do from the successes."

robindupont.com
@robindupontceramics

"I feel like a lot of us forget that we are our own bosses and that we can change things up if necessary, or if we want to. For example, if you don't like putting handles on and it's drudgery every time, then the handle usually shows that in some way. We forget that it is within our power to change. I think it is important to step outside of ourselves and change the rules. Take chances."

BOTH ARTIST AND MOTHER

KATE FISHER

A small shift in the everyday circumstances of our lives can lead us down new paths—where we might discover our purpose and passion. Kate Fisher was first introduced to clay at her high school, because art class was the only alternative to attending study hall. Years later, she has received a BA in both art history and studio arts, and an MFA in ceramics. Kate's passion for clay has grown exponentially since high school and it has opened the door to numerous adventures, such as research a trip to China. She is one of many who have been seduced by the colourful 20,000-year history of ceramics throughout the world, and the variety of firing processes an artist can use in their work. Specifically, Kate is drawn to the tradition of wood firing and its community-based approach to firing and labour.

Community is often foremost in Kate's thoughts—most visible in her contribution to the art community through her long-standing blog, Both Artist and Mother. This project, she says, "has manifested in articles, exhibitions and a group residency at Red Lodge Clay Center." Since 2013, Kate has collected interviews with artist-mothers on how they weave a professional life along with raising their children. Her own studio practice delves deep into themes of home and motherhood. "I absorb influences from all around me," says Kate. "This includes but is not limited to historical objects, contemporary practices and objects of aesthetic intrigue. Currently, my domestic landscape, full of haphazard child detritus and paraphernalia, is perpetually ripe for harvesting source material. My home is an endless fountain of ideas for forms, subject matter and surface treatment."

"Sturdy, bright and just right. I reflect my personality in my work by first and foremost knowing myself—flaws, attributes and all. I recognize that I am a conglomeration of my interests and experiences: mother, artist and athlete, to name a few. Like all humans, I am a paradox."

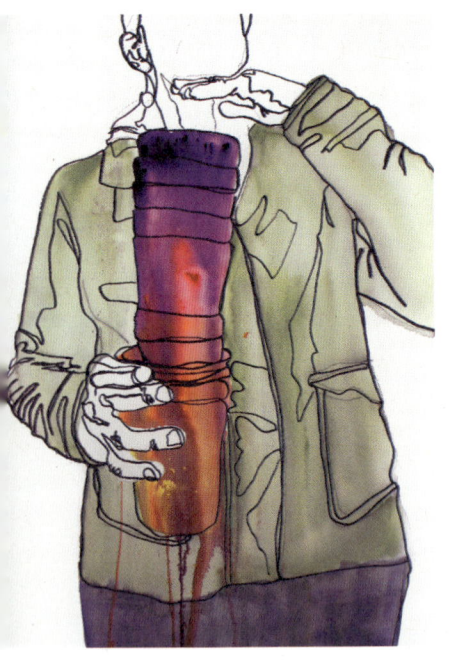

"I aim to discuss domestic objects and utility in my work. While the bulk of my creative practice is rooted in function, my practice takes tangents away from actual function into works that explore utility as a conceptual framework. I am repeatedly drawn to the home as a source for the beginnings of my investigation. The ever-changing landscape of home keeps me coming back to it as a place, for its familial relationships, and because of the objects it contains."

The functional nature of pottery and the connections it creates between people is central to Kate's work. She is unyielding in her belief that utilitarian objects have, as she says, "the power to impact people in meaningful ways." She explains: "Working with my hands to create a metaphorical handshake between the maker and the user, I constantly examine, respect and honour utility, even when developing contemplative or sculptural forms. I am drawn to the domestic environment through personal artifacts, repetitious rituals and intimate relationships. Home, whether the structure or the geographic location, can evoke specific feelings and memories. I enjoy embracing and expressing both the permanent and the ephemeral qualities of what we think of as home. The act of living and creating artwork that stems from these notions dissolves the boundaries between my home and my studio. It fuses the home with the studio and creates an all-encompassing life aesthetic."

ENDLESS POSSIBILITIES

The range of creative possibilities in ceramics is endless. Each clay body provides new variations on colour and texture. Each style of firing defines aesthetics. In the studio, Kate does not play favourites. "I have worked with a variety of clays, firing temperatures and kiln styles," she says. "I purposely choose to not be a kiln monogamist, but rather faithful to a firing temperature. I appreciate the variation I can achieve through different kilns and enjoy this variety in my creative practice. This gives me the flexibility to fire kilns with various communities and friends. The ability to engage with others through firing is important to me and my work." ❉

"I stand at the edge of the diving board. I envision the ideal dive. I imagine what could go wrong. I imagine what could go right. I think about how the water will feel on my body. I wait until I can no longer handle the anticipation and then I jump. The same is true in my studio practice. The wait at the end of the board takes many shapes: sketchbook, visual research, writing, reading. In the end it is the leap (or repetition of leaps) that makes the new work possible."

MOVING FORWARD

It can be hard to find the mental space for research, new work, experimentation and play when one has to maintain a studio practice, job responsibilities and domestic commitments. Like most mothers, Kate is constantly on the go—creative ideas often form at unexpected times and intervals. While she would love to be the type of artist who fills sketchbooks to the brim with drawings and notes, most of the time Kate is simply drafting thoughts and words into a 99-cent notepad that she carries in her pocket.

Kate makes sure she carves out time to participate in sports, something that has been integral in her life since she swam competitively as a child. "The hard work, dedication, repetition and commitment to stroke efficiently have shaped who I am as an artist and person," she says. Nowadays she is more likely to be found biking, running or skiing. Kate values these solo times. "These activities unexpectedly or unintentionally give me the mental space to filter various thoughts about my life and practice."

fisherclay.com
@fishclay

PERENNIAL CREATIVITY

DEBRA KUZYK & RAY MACKIE

Nestled beside the farmers market in Annapolis Royal, a seaside town in Nova Scotia, you will find a bright yellow building that is home to Lucky Rabbit Pottery. Walk through the doorway and you'll be inside one of Canada's most colourful and vibrant pottery showrooms, that of Debra Kuzyk and her husband, Ray Mackie. The couple has sold work out of this space for 21 years. They also used to live here and had their studio in the building. "There is an old model of living above the shop, in a good location and working on street level," says Debra. "That's

"Ray and I have been supporting ourselves with our production for over 20 years. We combined a pottery retail outlet with an exhibition career: pottery in the summer, studio production and exhibition in the winter and spring."

what we did. Our studios were in the back, and the pottery shop was in the front corner. We raised a family there. It was tight but economical."

"The pottery and tile work is accessible to our customer base of locals, tourists and summer visitors," she explains. "Because I sell it myself in the shop, I receive continuous feedback, which is a mostly positive experience for me. The exhibition work allows us to push our limits, explore our passions and supposedly slow down a little. When an exhibition is over, I bring the work to the shop and sell it from there." Debra notes that they do have serious collectors. "This way of working evolved from living in a summer tourist destination. Winter is the time we have to explore larger work, apply for exhibitions and research new materials and techniques to satisfy our artistic ambitions. We also have a chance to build up a little inventory for the summer months."

Debra and Ray have supported themselves for over two decades with their production work, the retail outlet beside the farmers market and the recent addition of a tile shop that Debra says allows her to "sell reproductions of my own work in an authentic and affordable way." While they do hire some help, Debra is also the labourer behind the retail and administrative end of the business—"Ray is good with chemistry, kilns, photography and technical problems."

Now that their kids are grown, Debra and Ray have moved their household out of the bright yellow building and have established a new home and individual studio spaces away from their retail space. "I no longer own the building but am a tenant in the space I created," says Debra. "From the sale of the building, Ray and I were able to buy a home outside of town and pay off our debts." Before selling, the couple renovated the original studio so that it could house four ateliers: for pottery, tiles, jewellery and handmade bags. "It took three years to achieve this final form of the artist collective, but it was worth it!" The Lucky Rabbit Pottery building is now home to this artist collective, with the inclusion of two other craft artists. "This allows us to support one another and cooperate on retail

"I define success by the amount of contentment I feel in my day-to-day life." —Debra

endeavours. It brings more people and offers them a diverse experience. People love to see us at work."

They are proud of the destination they have created through hard work and creativity. "This market is the heart and soul of the community and a destination for summer visitors," Debra says. "We just open the front door and we are part of it!"

Debra attributes their longevity and sustainability to the fact that they remain adaptable as a business and play an active role in the local community. "We have survived a few serious challenges: health troubles, economic crisis and this year the coronavirus. We are small and stay adaptable. We can respond to a local request, design a cup for the coffee shop, tile the mantle for the local restaurant. We are part of the community. I donate to fundraisers and volunteer my time, and this has a reciprocal effect." ✽

"Ray makes the forms he likes and presents them to me. He likes to keep things loose and mixed up, so we usually don't make sets or replicas of our own designs. I like to make multiples or groupings of pieces that will work together, each with a slight variation—like a team in matching shirts."

lucky-rabbit-pottery.com
@deb_kuzyk

CREATIVE PARTNERSHIP.

What is interesting about Lucky Rabbit Pottery is how Debra and Ray divide the tasks in making their wares. Ray throws all the pieces for Debra to decorate, brings them to her wet for her to work on, and then takes them back to complete the cycle of glazing and firing.

With each artist respecting the other, the creative partnership functions well. "He never tells me what to do, and vice versa," says Debra. "We are both content with our own role, and Ray prefers to remain behind the scenes."

During the wet clay stage, Debra models the figures for the tops of lidded jars, carves the surface of the clay forms and sgraffito carves her illustrations through layers of underglaze. The narratives of the work truly come to light in the carving process. It is the stage Debra calls "a beautiful, relaxing, seductive process."

Years ago, Debra and Ray broke away from the Nova Scotia pottery trend of working in local red earthenware. Instead, they work with a more durable cone six white clay body, which they cover in dark colours for sgraffito design. This unique style has allowed them to stand apart and has helped grow their business. "I gravitate to vibrant colours or black-and-white graphics, with strong ties to ceramic history," Debra says.

In winter months, when their tourist town is quieter, the artists can devote more time to experimentation and exhibition work, on top of production wares.

LINEAGE IN CLAY

SHED POTTERY

Born and raised in the stunning landscape of the Niagara region of Ontario, Johann Munro has nature in her bones and a hard work ethic in her blood. Because her formative years were spent in this landscape, swimming in backyard creeks and learning the value of community and creativity, Johann has built her own dream life and job in the region. "I have always felt a strong connection to the land and nature, especially that of Niagara," she says. "We have beautifully lush forests and parks that run alongside the escarpment. Niagara is known for wine and hospitality. It's a flourishing region with hardworking folk." Her business, shed pottery, perfectly complements the tourist region. Johann is half of shed pottery alongside Ryan Byng, her partner in life and work.

Johann's beginning in clay and pottery can be attributed to her grandmother, Jean Garriock. At a time in her twenties when she was feeling without purpose or direction, Jean taught Johann how to throw on the potter's wheel.

"My grandmother was a potter," writes Johann in a loving tribute to her grandmother, posted on the shed pottery website. "Toward the back of her property next to the raspberry bush sat her little blue shed. Every time I slept over at grandma's house I would grab the key with the whistle attached to it and venture out to her shed. Even though her shed wasn't very big I would find myself lost in there for hours. Her shelves were filled with mason jars of powders, marbles, glass bits, sand, sea foam sponges and other curious things. An old wooden kick wheel sat pressed up against the wall. It was archaic and clunky, a tool that she never used but never parted with."

"Focusing on functional wares was born out of necessity and is something I have grown to appreciate. Functional is not boring; it's an incredible honour to make wares for people to enjoy in their daily rituals and lives."
—Johann

"I am a true minimalist at heart; clutter overwhelms me and busies my mind. I like to live quietly and peacefully. I think that the need for a quiet mind and a happy heart is reflected in the work I create. No piece is ever too detailed or overwhelming. The shapes are comfortable and the palette is natural and calming."

Johann often spent hours in the dirt basement of Jean's home, opening her mind to the ability of clay, creativity and the handmade to provide focus and purpose in one's life. "When I finally would surface hours later with a small overworked pot, I would feel lighter and happier," Johann says. "I expressed this to my grandmother with a big smile on my face and she would say, "that's because clay is good for your head."

Almost a decade later, Johann decided to pursue a creative path full time. "In 2014, I changed paths from working in the hospitality industry to become a full-time potter. It wasn't a decision I made consciously. The story of how I became a brick-and-mortar proprietor and full-time ceramist happened organically. It is a story that started with a bump in the road followed by a dream, coupled with a little fate, a great deal of hard work and tears, the support of our community, and a husband who was willing to join me on this wild ride."

OPENING UP SHOP

Having had informal training through workshops and residencies, then making pottery on the side and selling at local markets, Johann was in many ways prepared for this new venture. "I decided to throw a sign out by the road that read 'pottery open,'" she says. "Soon after taking this leap I received a call from a local chef looking to have dishes made for his upcoming cookbook, which I fulfilled. From there, one connection led to another and I was eventually making thousands of wares for several local restaurants and breweries."

WOOD AND SODA KILNS

"Ryan once referred to my work as 'modern country,' and that description continues to fit. The pots we make can sometimes be primitive by design; some wares are reminiscent of a rusty weathered surface, and other collections reflect a soft palette on a refined form—a perfect balance between modern (contemporary) and country (rustic)." Johann and Ryan achieve this aesthetic through wood and soda firing at their home-based studio and gallery. Because it is a country property, there is room for all the kilns that require weeks of work to fill, days to fire and an equal amount of days to cool before unloading. "I love firing our wood kiln. I wish we could get to it more often, but the making cycles are long. The firing process is so thrilling and primitive. To know we are influencing the surface of our pots with every log we throw is a magical emotion—of course, one that is also balanced with science, but the entire process is enchanting and exhausting." ❉

"When art feels like work we acknowledge our path and remind ourselves that this is a beautiful opportunity to be able to create, and to create together for others. We try to wake each morning with grateful hearts so we don't lose sight of our dream."

BALANCING BUSINESS

The gallery side of the business has been around since 2014, and in 2017 Ryan quit his job to join Johann in the business full time. The gallery shop is a renovated part of their home in which they also sell the work of other artists in the region. Johann and Ryan balance the different aspects of the studio and the business well. Limiting their open hours to two days a week allows them more concentrated studio time so they can fill the many shelves of the wood kiln. Johann takes on the administrative duties and oversees the creative direction of the shop and the brand. Ryan, meanwhile, brings his integral knowledge of science to his role as studio technician, as well as potter.

shedpotterybyjohann.com
@shedpottery

BUSINESS TIPS

Be a risk-taker. "You need to be a risk-taker; you need to be motivated and hard-working. You need to be a little dose of crazy also. Life as a full-time potter is taxing on your body and can leave you with little time for a life outside of clay, but it is a tremendously rewarding life and one that you can never take for granted."

Be organized. "It's really important to be organized. You need to have a sense for business, such as an understanding of profit and loss, marketing, self-worth, niche opportunities and relationship building with your audience."

Prioritize. "We have made our business our lifestyle. It can be draining physically and creatively, but prioritizing balance between work and personal time has helped to ensure we can stay fresh and motivated. Accepting that our turnaround time is slow and educating others on the process has helped to ensure we maintain healthy minds and bodies. We no longer put our pots first, although they do and will always play a leading role in our daily life."

FUNCTIONAL / POLITICAL

JUSTIN ROTHSHANK

It is a common thread woven through the stories of many functional studio potters: an upbringing in which handmade objects were valued and family dinner tables were set with beautifully crafted pottery. Justin Rothshank is one of those artists who looks back fondly on those early lessons in craftsmanship and sees how they have shaped his philosophy as a maker. "When I was a child, my family always ate off of handmade pottery," he recalls. He remembers his parents including him on visits to local potters to select the objects that would play a part in their daily mealtime.

Justin's high school art teacher was also instrumental in setting him on his path in ceramics. In fact, she was so supportive and aware of his potential that she arranged for him at that young age to fire a wood kiln alongside some local artists. The process of firing a wood kiln is very community orientated. There are many tasks to undertake in preparation of the firing and the kiln requires many days to pack, to fire and to cool down before it can be opened and the treasures within unveiled. The draw of this type of involvement, to contributing as part of a team towards a common goal, continues to fuel Justin's excitement in the studio.

Collaboration in the studio helps keep Justin's work fresh and evolving. He shares his studio space with his wife, Brooke, who is a well-known painter, and with his children, as well as with a handful of interns. Through collaboration, Justin has extended his talents into the mediums of hot glass, metal jewellery and wood. "Through collaboration, I've learned about broader firing temperatures for ceramic decals, new connections to material manufacturers and much

"My goal is to be a potter for my career. I work to produce pots that are contemporary and timeless. I constantly test, write, research, share and connect with others about my work. I want to innovate and stay relevant while continuing to make tableware that is high quality and interesting to a large audience."

"In contemporary ceramics, surface is everything. I fit in because I love working with surface through decals, glazes, firing processes, drawing and more. Layering surfaces is at the heart of what I do."

more," he says. "Collaboration has been enormously important from both a research perspective and a business perspective. As a self-employed artist, experimentation in creative work is important, but experimentation in marketing, networking and outreach is equally important."

Collaborations for Justin and Brooke extend beyond the studio into the community. Over the last three years, they have combined forces to work on gratitude projects. In 2019 this was the Sharing Intention project. Brooke illustrated designs for ceramic decals, based on words of intention that they discussed each week throughout the year. They created fifty-two pieces. These decals eventually make their way onto fired works, and through social media are finding their ways into the hands of strangers throughout the United States. As artists, Justin and Brooke hope that these objects of beauty and contemplation will spark dialogue in new communities, help build relationships and inspire intentional living.

GUARDIANS OF THE LAND

Justin and his family are devoted to the land on which they live and work. They bought an untouched piece of woodland in Goshen, Indiana, in 2009. They built all of the buildings that are now on the property using the resources of the land around them. Justin is keenly aware that it is impossible to exist in nature without some sort of human footprint that forever alters the landscape, but the protection of this land is of great concern to him. No development proceeds without careful and considered planning.

This consideration of the land also comes into play with Justin's wood firings. He harvests deadfall from the acres around the kiln. As the trees turn to ash in the kiln, they literally become the decoration on the pottery surfaces. The ash is carried by flame through the kiln, landing on the clay surfaces at such high temperatures that the ash turns to glaze. Not all of his pottery is fired in this manner; however, all of the kilns on the property are fuel-efficient, as Justin makes many technical choices based on ecological sustainability.

Justin's functional pottery is inspired by both the natural world around him and his passion for social justice. "In making this work, I've reflected on the beauty, inspiration and energy that the environment provides to me—the wildlife, changing seasons, flora and fauna, fuel and resource," he explains. "Yet I recognize that we've changed the natural environment significantly since our arrival on this land. I make this work as a reminder of the responsibility I carry in preserving the natural environment, educating those around me and understanding the history that impacts the present and the future."

"I'm interested in creating pieces that suggest narrative and story. I want pieces to be picked up, turned around, held and used. When preparing the surface, and decorating, I try to create marks and designs that encourage users to rotate the piece. I want to drive the eye around the form, hide subtle surprises in detail within the design, and leave space for the viewer to breathe and relax within the design."

NEWS RADIO AND POLITICAL POTTERY

News radio is the soundtrack to Justin's studio life. Streaming into his studio are the lives, struggles and situations of others around the world. Consequently, his functional pottery pieces become objects of immense emotional and moral weight. "The issues I address, through imagery, form and surface, impact us all, regardless of our individual political persuasions," he says. "Current events impact my political work. I also make pottery depicting politicians from our history, and floral imagery that represents remembrance and honour for those who have served, my opposition to war, and my interest in working towards positive social change through relationship building." The pacificism of his Mennonite heritage flows through all of his work at some level.

AUTHOR AND MORE

Making functional studio pottery is only one component of Justin's artistic and professional practice. He is also an internationally published writer, and has travelled extensively in the US and abroad as a presenter, panelist, visiting artist and artist in residence. In 2020 he published a book on low-fire soda firing, the first of its kind on the subject and the product of extensive research over a 10-year period into the atmospheric firing of earthenware. ✻

rothshank.com
@jrothshank

CREATIVE PROCESS

"I make lots of pots, working in series," describes Justin. "Pots are decorated quickly, in small steps. Many small steps lead to the finished product. It's hard to explain the process for all my work because I use a broad variety of processes. I work with earthenware, stoneware and porcelain. At any given time there could be six different clay bodies in use in my studio. I work with a broad range of glazes, including low fire, cone three, cone six and cone ten glazes. There are more than 15 different glazes that are part of my regular processes. I fire pots in a variety of different kilns, including electric, gas-fired soda and wood-fired. What binds the work together is the final step, of refiring using ceramic decals. I have a massive decal library that includes many different floral images, a large collection of images I have designed and custom ordered, and a large collection of political icon imagery that I've created."

Refiring and reworking his pottery pieces until he is happy with them helps to keep objects out of the landfill. "Boring surfaces, glaze flaws and decal imperfections are all failures that I can fix by refiring," he says. "This multi-firing process has led to much more complexity in my surface designs, and opportunities to create depth of field within the glazed surface."

WEARABLE ART AND CULTURE

HADIYA WILLIAMS

When the world seems at its most unsettled, artists and creatives really get to work. This was the case for Hadiya Williams, from Washington, DC, and how she discovered a new creative passion—ceramics. "I signed up for a two-hour workshop with a friend in February 2017," explains Hadiya. "It was right after the inauguration and I was definitely looking for distractions. We'd been talking about doing something creative with our hands." Hadiya took to ceramics immediately, and effortlessly.

Her formal education and professional work in computer science, graphic design and art direction laid the foundation for ceramics—and for her goal of developing a creative lifestyle brand. "I spent a lot of time trying to find my voice through my graphic design work," she says. "I developed a distinct style but I always knew that my design was best suited for craftwork." Her visually bold graphic ceramics are but one of the products in her creative line of textiles, apparel and paper goods, sometimes imagined through collaborations with other makers.

What began as a social clay workshop quickly lead Hadiya to seek out accessible options for further learning. "YouTube, Pinterest, Skillshare, Creativebug—I was all over the place trying to learn. I eventually enrolled in some community ceramics classes at a few local DC studios." Her current studio includes a small eight-by-eight-inch kiln, which, while limiting the scale of her work, does not limit its potential. "Limitations can breed creativity," says Hadiya, and this kiln-size limitation has led to her distinctive, one-of-a-kind line of wearable art. "I am thankful for

"The adaptable nature of clay, the texture and the blank slate makes it a perfect medium for exploring cultural memory—shaping and reshaping, physically, through the moulding of the clay, and abstractly, through the visual relationship of these items to the past."

"Because my world is centred around Black women across the diaspora and I am one of these women, I am creating work that I'd wear or that is inspired by architecture or textiles, or ancient and cultural artwork that has inspired me over the years. My personal style has been pretty consistent as long as I can remember. It's my execution that has evolved."

how accessible ceramics has been. My work is simple but it includes a lot of experimentation. It's like a playground for me. I try not to take the creation process too seriously or else I lose the ability to come up with new ideas."

The material properties of clay and its historical connections have long been of interest to Hadiya, even if her own experimentation in ceramics is more recent. Collecting handmade and vintage works in clay to surround herself with over the years has, perhaps subconsciously, worked as a research study of what styles and objects inspire her stylistically. Her deep appreciation of materials and textures is clear in each object she makes for her collection. "My subject matter is always centred around the culture of the African diaspora," she explains. "Creating handmade objects with clay that are wearable, functional or for display allows me to tell these short visual stories with each piece."

Hadiya describes her artistic style as being modern yet classic, global yet self-aware: "The lines and shapes are simple and flawed and bold. There are

textures and layers as well. This is definitely reflective of me and my personal style." Hadiya's acclaimed aesthetic leanings originate in her childhood and with the art and books her mother would surround her with, including the illustrations of Leo and Diane Dillon in *The People Could Fly* and the social messages portrayed in the gripping, light and dark stylized illustrations of Elizabeth Catlett. Although Hadiya's work itself is not figurative, it references "architecture or textiles, or ancient and cultural artwork." She notes the influence of batik textiles, mudcloth and African masks on her visual lexicon. "I grew up with African and Black art everywhere in my home."

Hadiya is currently focused on creating wearable art: "For me, it was also the most accessible place to start. I was eager to create, so I started with small shapes and forms, creating objects that I could seamlessly put to use. The pieces I make are ones I'd wear myself. I have created some pots, cups, bells, plates and other décor pieces and I plan to explore much more, but I truly love creating jewellery and wearable pieces. I feel like these small, almost two-dimensional surfaces showcase my design in the best way."

"I'm going to keep learning and trying so I can break the rules as much as possible." ✼

"I am essentially developing a lifestyle brand that involves ceramics as well as other functional pieces and artwork. My design style is used across a few mediums, so what I create will expand. Plus people love to adorn themselves and they will always appreciate handmade work."

"When I first started looking for ways that ceramics are made, I found some videos of women in Burkina Faso taking dirt from the ground and hand-building these huge pots with coils. I felt connected to that process."

blackpepperpaperie.com
@hadiyawilliams

CREATIVE STYLE

"My sketchbook is filled with new object ideas and black painted or hand-drawn lines and shapes," describes Hadiya, about preferring graphic designs. "Black-and-white has remained a constant since day one—it is timeless and a great neutral combination. I add colour here and there, but I love black-and-white matte glazes and underglazes." The designs that she paints and draws on paper are typically in the same style that she will paint or carve into ceramic pieces, but she also leaves room for experimentation and serendipity. "I'll just cut a shape freehand or use cutters and then let the form dictate the design. It ends up being an intuitive process. Because of this, most of my pieces are one of a kind."

Hadiya's favourite part of the process is the glaze kiln reveal. "I don't do much test tile work just because I work with basic colours and glazes, and I make small pieces. I know how they will fire for the most part. It really ends up being about the layout per se rather than the glazing. I love using black-and-white underglazes on speckled clay to achieve that uncoated, painted-on texture where the speckles show through." This cone six speckled clay has a natural brown colour and works well as a neutral base for her surface designs. "I appreciate that it feels and looks like it came from the earth."

LESS IS MORE

WRITTEN BY JULIA KRUEGER

NATALIE J WOOD

THE ART OF POETIC OBSERVATION

KALIKA BOWLBY

Golden, British Columbia, is a town nestled between six of Canada's national parks, and needless to say, the Rocky Mountain scenery is breathtaking. For Kalika Bowlby, who lives here with her family, this environment nourishes her creativity: "I am surrounded by wild mountains, forests and rivers, which provide constant reminders about being unencumbered in creating. I balance my time in the studio with all the ways to be in the mountains—hiking, biking and skiing, whatever the season allows. We have created a tiny little homestead on our plot of land, with fruit trees, grape vines, berry bushes and a big vegetable and flower garden. This provides nourishment and inspiration on so many levels. There is a deep, symbiotic relationship between kitchen, garden and studio." Although Kalika's environment is nothing short of spectacular and is a source for inspiration in her work, her aesthetic is poetically minimal, encouraging you to slow down, observe, notice and appreciate the subtleties in her work and in nature.

Kalika is a production potter who makes functional objects intended for daily use. From an early age, she was fascinated with forming shapes with clay that she had discovered at the edge of a creek running through her backyard. She initially enrolled in a studio-based program at the Kootenay School of the Arts (KSA) in Nelson, BC, which focused on building the hands-on skills necessary for running a studio. She then transferred to the Alberta College of Art and Design in Calgary, Alberta, where she had a chance "to put words to what I was doing and really question what I wanted to be doing with clay. This was easier to do thanks to the foundation of skills I built at KSA."

"The art of observation is an important part of my creative process. Noticing things in the world. When a shape or line is pleasing or colours play well off each other. Noticing what creates symmetry and interest. This can happen anywhere, with anything, in the natural world or the human-made landscape, but it is the noticing that is important."

Her studio is located on the bottom floor of her home and is equipped with an electric wheel, shelving and three large work tables. For Kalika, having a home-based studio is convenient, as it enables her to carefully attend to the time-sensitive parts of production work—drying and firing—in combination with the other demands of life. However, because she lives in a small town and her studio is home-based, there is a sense of being physically isolated from the larger community of ceramic artists—although the Internet and social media have enabled her to stay connected.

After the busy holiday season of production and selling, January is quite slow in the studio, so Kalika uses this time to explore new ideas. She finds that working in another medium, like painting or drawing, can sometimes help to shake things up by breaking habits and patterns formed during regular production. "I hold the question 'what if?' in my mind as I'm venturing into new terrain," she says. "It's essential for me to not feel pressure to share my explorations and experiments. I lower my expectations about posting

on social media and sharing what's happening in the studio. It allows me to let things evolve at their own pace rather than grasping at reaching a conclusion. Sometimes nothing concrete or specific comes out of this time, but I think it influences the coming year and can lead to evolution down the road." A sketchbook is essential when Kalika is exploring new ideas, as her minimalist aesthetic requires formal precision, and drawing is an efficient way to work out subtleties of form and possible variations. The second stage of "sketching" happens in clay, with scaled-down versions of her designs. As she does not own a test kiln, the smaller scale enables her to "sneak" experiments into her large kiln. She rarely fires a load of work that doesn't have at least one test or experiment in it.

At first glance, Kalika's vessels appear subtle and spare, but over time they reveal their variations in colour, texture and weight. Each pot is like a carefully composed poem in which every word, line and stanza is related, unfolding into a pleasurable aesthetic experience. And just like a good poem, her pots can

"I have a minimalist aesthetic. I focus on simplicity and functionality because the objects will in some ways be the backdrop. Eventually, they will hold or contain things— tea, coffee, breakfast or dinner. I express through the colour and form, with a goal of finding a sense of harmony and balance in each object. I suppose this is a reflection of my personality and a broader goal of living in harmony with the world around me."

change how you see, understand and connect to the world. "Making functional objects relates to my interests in food and slow living," Kalika explains. "The art in many ways is in the experience. The user becomes part of the process and their experience of weight, texture and subtlety is important. It is intimate, and as a maker I find meaning in considering all the aspects of a potential user's experience." Observing and appreciating the subtleties in Kalika's work makes you want to look to her inspirations as well: architecture, historical ceramics, her garden and the environment around her. Suddenly, the quieter colours pop—the blushes of purple and rose found in an alpine meadow, or on freshly harvested asparagus from her garden or in a bouquet of flowers—and the more intense colours fall away. You find yourself asking, "How did I never notice how purple asparagus really is? What else am I not noticing?" Time and a sense of being unfold differently when the delicate blushes of life come to the forefront, garnering a deeper, more poetic appreciation for life on Earth beyond the spectacle of thundering waterfalls, herds of big game and fields of bright red poppies. This sense of slow, poetic observation and appreciation is what defines Kalika's work: "I suppose this is a reflection of my personality and a broader goal of living in harmony with the world around me." ❈

"There's a desire to have things in our lives that have a trace of the human hand and express the creativity and beauty that humans are capable of. Of course, we no longer 'need' handmade objects. But we do need to feel connected. Handmade objects can provide an antidote to the standardization of an increasingly technological world."

"I want all the details to complement each other and not be in competition."

KALIKA BOWLBY

SUSTAINABLE BUSINESS

Kalika supports herself as a production studio potter and also occasionally teaches workshops. Making, however, is only one aspect of running a small business. Also part of the mix is repairing and maintaining equipment; photography for marketing, social media and website updates; replying to emails; applying for grants; speaking and writing about her pots; bookkeeping; and packing and shipping her wares. It could be easy to feel overwhelmed by all these tasks and the constant attention they require, but Kalika finds it satisfying. "This diversity is partly what keeps things interesting for me," she says. Being able to work alone and being self-motivated and well-organized is key.

Even with such a full plate, sustainability is an integral part of Kalika's practice and business. Thinking sustainably can encompass the financial, physical, environmental, social and emotional parts of her job. In terms of economic sustainability, for example, she sells her work through a variety of markets (craft councils, galleries, handmade markets, retail shops and online) in order to make her business less susceptible to fluctuations in the economy. The physical demands of a ceramics practice have caused Kalika to think sustainably as well: "I had carpal tunnel surgery a couple years ago. It made me realize that for my business to be physically sustainable I needed to incorporate better practices, and overwork is not really an option. This has led me to restructure my studio practice somewhat, with longevity in mind."

kalikabowlby.com
@kalikabowlby

CHANCE AND CONTROL

JACKIE FRIOUD

"Although I strive for the perfect pot, it is always out of reach, and that keeps my quest fresh, creative and adventurous."

Making has always been an important part of Jackie Frioud's life. She studied art at the postsecondary level but came to clay after her kids started school, when she "was itching to make things." She took a ceramics course at her local community centre and discovered her love for combining design and function into practical objects. This discovery led to several years of study with Sam Kwan at Capilano College in Vancouver, British Columbia, where she learned the atmospheric technique of salt firing. Her salt glazed functional wares are minimal in design but full of process and tactility, creating a balanced tension within her work. "I work towards a tension between chance and control," Jackie states, "paring down my forms in search of a perfect shape and proportion, but allowing the process to show in the subtle marks and gestures of my hands, the trail of the flame and the salt vapour, and the inherent qualities of clay."

The quest for a perfectly controlled form anchors Jackie's practice. Inspired by function—or by a space in the kiln that needs filling—she begins a new design by drawing loosely in her sketchbook until one or two designs stand out. She then moves to the wheel to work on shape, pairing it down to its formal essentials. "My favourite part of the process is taking the thrown parts and putting them together," she says. "The more complicated the piece the better. I love making my oval oil bottles—they have six parts that need to fit together. I love that quiet process of fitting, rasping, scraping and paddling, making sure everything looks balanced and feels good in the hand." She adds detail to her pots through the addition of handles, subtle ribbed lines, simple feet and rims, and bands of applied slip, which

work with the underlying clay body to produce various colours and textures, ranging from dry to shiny to orange peel–like and glossy smooth. Salt glazing adds an "earthy aesthetic that enhances the simple forms," Jackie says. "I guess I have a need for a certain amount of control, which shows in the forms, but the salt glazing tempers that part of my nature, introducing some randomness to keep things surprising."

Four years ago, Jackie moved from a home-based studio with a salt kiln on site into a rented studio in East Vancouver in a building dedicated to artist studios. She shares the space with five other female ceramic artists: "I've really enjoyed getting to know other artists, troubleshooting with them as things come up, and generally having company once in a while," she says. "If we were all there working, it would definitely be tight, but that never happens. Our building has lots of ceramicists working in it, so that is a wonderful larger community, too." They all share the big work tables, electric kilns, spray booth and glazing areas, but they also have their own spaces. Jackie generally works alone when making her vessels and is in the studio four or five days a week.

She salt-fires her pots five or six times a year and has to travel five hours and take two ferries to get to her kiln at the Tidal Art Centre in Lund, BC. Before making the trip, she slips and bisques all her pots at the Vancouver studio. She transports them stacked in totes and wraps each piece in a few layers of dry cleaning plastic so that if they rub up against each other during the journey, the surfaces won't be marked. She describes the salt firing process in Lund as immersive and full: "When I go to fire, I am immersed in a community of creative people as well as natural beauty. I spend five days travelling, firing and waiting for the kiln to cool—a lovely interlude of hiking, socializing and swimming in the summer. So though I miss my former studio, kiln and home, I have new connections to other artists and that is wonderful." Her work might be minimal but Jackie's practice is teeming with process and community, and her atmospheric firings add an element of uncontrollability to her controlled forms.

THE KILN

Since 2001, Jackie has been dedicated to salt glazing. "I was so lucky to find salt firing early in my practice," she says. "I have been focussed on making work that is enhanced by that process." She built her first kiln in 2007 at her former home-based studio and in 2017 built a new kiln at the Tidal Art Centre in Lund. Salt glazing first emerged in 15th century Germany, and at the time, it revolutionized European ceramics, which were mainly lead-glazed earthenware. Some believe that salt glazing was "discovered" after the wood from old salted herring barrels was used for fuel, although this has yet to be proven. No matter its start, salt glazing was so revolutionary because it created a highly durable, non-porous body that could be used for the transportation, storage and drinking of liquids, for preservation and for pharmaceutical and sanitary uses, including sewer pipes.

When salt is added during the firing process, it vaporizes and spreads throughout the kiln, making the kiln and its design especially important. The sodium reacts with the silica found in clay, creating a glassy, glazed surface with a texture that resembles an orange peel. Potters today get to know their kilns and pack them strategically to obtain certain results. As Jackie says, "having my own kilns has allowed me to continue to tweak the firings and saltings to suit my aesthetic. The quantity of salt I use, the placement of work in the kiln, the treatment of the surface texture and choice of clays and slips are all considered." ❋

"Clay teaches us to accept that things don't always work out—it's a good life lesson!"

jackiefrioud.com
@jackie_frioud_pottery

SELLING

Jackie sells most of her work through studio tour events, craft fairs or home sales. "In the past, I have sold by consignment or wholesale through some wonderful shops and galleries," she says. "However, I find it difficult to make a consistent line of work for these outlets and find that my independent sales opportunities are less stressful and I can keep 100% of the sales." She tends to avoid taking on commissions unless there is leeway in the finished piece. "It's more important to have the freedom to follow my interests than to try to match someone else's expectations. Also, with salt glazing, it's hard to replicate something exactly."

THE INVISIBLE HAND

NORIKO MASUDA

"My work is my way of making connections with people, so I want to consider others."

The hand is everywhere in craft and ceramics: close-up shots of romanticized, hardworking hands, traces of the hand left on the surfaces of pots, and countless references to "the hand" in ceramics-related literature. With the hand comes its opposite, the machine, and this can lead to binary thinking and unnecessary divisions between craft, industry and design. Take Noriko Masuda's impeccably precise table, tea and homewares, which show no signs of the hand, even though they are handmade. Her "invisible hand" is purposeful: "My work is sometimes mistaken to be machine made, or even mass-produced. Some can't see the 'maker's hand,' the process marks, in my work. But my process, my 'hand,' is that very lack of an obvious mark."

Noriko was born in Japan, and her family moved to Canada when she was just one year old. She grew up in Calgary, Alberta, and recalls "eating Japanese food in the way that my parents were familiar with: small dishes of various shapes and sizes dotting the table. Many of my forms are based on those dinner tables. My strongest influence is my Japanese background." She worked for just under 10 years in her father's dental lab as a dental technician. "I enjoyed the making and the detail, but it didn't go well—the dental lab industry is extremely dependent on the economy," she says. "I decided that if I was going to struggle doing something I wasn't passionate about, I should struggle doing what I was passionate about instead. So I went back to school for ceramics. It was a good decision." At first, she attended classes at a community studio, then enrolled in the Australian National University's Distance Diploma program, and continued on with

graduate studies in the Ceramic Design Program at Staffordshire University in Stoke-on-Trent, UK. Noriko describes the program as being "purely about functional ware and is immersed in the ceramics industry. Our critique questions could be, Will this sell? How much does it cost to make? How much time will it take to make?"

Handcrafted precision in conjunction with a strong minimal aesthetic as well as industrial design and knowhow defines Noriko's practice. It is methodical and considered. "I am extremely slow," she says. "Ideas come slowly and I'm a slow maker." She does not keep a sketchbook, nor does she put images up in her studio. "It feels cluttered to me and stresses me out. But when I start a series, I do start a folder on my computer with images of particular ideas." She also uses CAD software when initially designing her work. However, the digital design is adjusted on the spot, as the plaster models are crafted using a plaster-turning lathe and bench whirler. These industrial tools are used to create symmetrical forms and smooth, even

surfaces. Her spout and handle models are either hand carved in plaster or 3D printed in ABS plastic; these smaller parts must be precise and symmetrical so as to avoid warping. The models are then used to create plaster slip casting moulds.

"I really enjoy the plaster stage as well, making both the models and the moulds," Noriko explains. "I get totally engrossed in making the models on the lathe. It's another form of throwing in a way. I can make a cylinder of plaster into a cup or teapot or vase form, and it feels so fresh at that stage. I often get a little carried away with the moulds as well. The inside is the critical part, but I spend far too much time making the outside of the moulds pristine and beautiful. There is just something so satisfying about a clean, smooth, new mould." Once the moulds are complete, Noriko slip casts her vessels using a brilliant white bone china casting slip and glazes them with commercially available glazes, giving her the bright, consistent colour quality she is looking for.

Although Noriko's minimal work does not overtly

"I'm very concerned about the ease of use of my pots and I design them with the user in mind. I relate it a little to my years as a dental technician. Crowns need to look and function as real teeth and never harm the patient. My work needs to fit within the users' lives, never make the user work to use them, and yet still be beautiful objects."

celebrate the "hand" with gestural marks and fingerprints, her invisible hand is ever-present—her process involves so much handwork, from plaster model making to slip casting, glazing and finishing—and when others pick up and use her carefully considered designs, multiple hands become part of the story. As attested by Noriko's work, the visible hand alone does not define the field of ceramics: design and industry combined with a precise, considered (in)visible hand is just as much a part of ceramics as well.

BONE CHINA

Noriko's wares obtain their brilliant white body from her casting with her own bone china slip—"bone" refers to the bone ash (made from calcined animal bones) that is added to the slip. It is no surprise she was introduced to bone china while studying in England, as this type of porcelain was formulated there in the 18th century: first at the Bow porcelain factory, then later refined by Josiah Spode in Stoke-on-Trent. In addition to its high level of whiteness, it is translucent and strong, making it ideal for tableware, and consequently it is associated with industrially produced ceramics. From a material standpoint, this historical association with industry complements Noriko's "invisible hand" aesthetic.

The material, however, is a challenge to work with, as it tends to slump and warp, and Noriko takes this into account during the design process. "My models need to look a little different from what I imagine the finished product to be," she says. "I need to include compensation curves, which can make the models look odd. I always fire one test piece from the first moulds to check that I'm getting what I want. If not, it's back to making changes on the model and making new moulds." In order to alleviate warping during the bisque fire, she fires most of her pieces on a bone china "setter" so that they keep their shape. "Essentially, I make two pieces for every one." To add to the challenges associated with this clay body, bone china is bisqued high and fired low. "This makes it quite awkward, as I'm glazing a vitrified object that doesn't absorb the liquid in the glaze." Consequently, Noriko sprays all her glazes in three layers, and finds that the pink tint in her commercial glaze enables her to see where she has sprayed. That said, for her, the brilliant white quality of the final product outweighs all the challenges. ❋

"I'm happiest making ceramics. If I can continue that, I would consider myself successful. If I'm making, I hope that means that people are enjoying my pieces, which would add more importance."

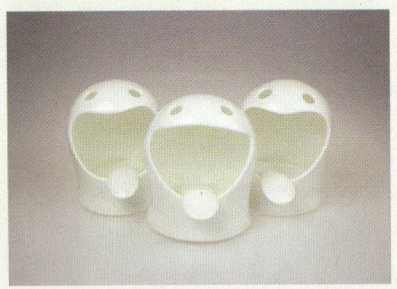

MEDALTA

In addition to her practice, Noriko is the residency coordinator of the Medalta international artists in residence program and a permanent resident at Medalta as well. "In general, I work four days a week for Medalta and I try to spend two days of the weekend in my own studio, or working on other aspects of my practice."

Medalta is an industrial museum, art gallery, contemporary ceramic art facility and community hub located in the 150-acre Historic Clay District of Medicine Hat, Alberta. Described on its website as "an exciting place where cutting-edge technologies meet historic restoration and archaeology," it features converted Medalta Potteries factory buildings (in operation under various names from 1912 to 1966), the 1938 and 1947 Hycroft China factory and warehouse buildings, a decommissioned brickyard, beehive kilns, archaeological excavations and artist studios. The international artist in residence program—ranging in duration from one day to a year—is designed for artists at all stages of

their career, and also includes an opportunity to teach in Medalta's education program. Noriko manages the administrative side of the residency with grant writing, programming and engaging with the resident artists, including through various community building activities.

The centre can accommodate up to 16 artists at one time and features movable walls so that spaces can cater to specific needs. Artists have 24-hour access to decal and silkscreening equipment, a glaze lab and spray booth, a plaster area for mould making, slab rollers and numerous electric, gas and atmospheric kilns.

One of the perks for Noriko of working for Medalta is that her studio is located on site in the 12,000-square-foot contemporary ceramics studio. Staff studios are on the second floor and set apart from the resident artist's studio. "It's a cozy space that I've made as private as possible," Noriko says. "This space is where I do my making of actual pieces—slip casting, cleaning casts, underglazing, sanding, etc. I also have a wheel there and shelving full of models and moulds."

medalta.org

norikomasuda.com
@norikomasuda

MINIMAL BUT VARIED

NATALIE J WOOD

Natalie J Wood grew up in Kirkcaldy, Scotland. "Kirkcaldy has a deep industrial history that was pretty much gone by the time I was born," she recalls. "It is famous for Linoleum and still has the last linen works in Scotland. It was also home to many potteries, the last of which closed around 90 years ago. I recently discovered that one of my great, great grandfathers worked as a kiln man for one of the potteries. My mum worked in a store that sold tiles, and as a child I would run up and down the aisles looking at all the different varieties. So in a way, I feel like ceramics is somewhat of a family business." Natalie completed a degree in three-dimensional design (ceramics) in 2015 from Gray's School of Art in Aberdeen, Scotland, and currently runs Natalie J Wood Designs out of Edinburgh. Rich, saturated colours and crisp, minimal forms define Natalie's functional wares, but her practice is far from "minimal," as she is constantly learning, embarking upon new ventures and actively collaborating with others.

As a self-described curious person with a love for learning, Natalie was drawn to the unlimited potential of ceramics. After finishing her university studies, she completed a micro-residency with Cyan Clayworks in Edinburgh and recently took part in Craft Scotland's Compass program. The program paired her with two mentors: William Gibson and Helen Voce. "William helped me in understanding more about the business side of running a studio and Helen has helped me develop and define my artistic practice and what I plan to do in the future," Natalie says. This program also encouraged her to reflect on her business, and to realize "that play and experimentation are incredibly

"People are attracted to the minimalist style and unusual colour palette of my pieces. My work has a dual purpose of being beautiful and functional, and in today's society, with people living smaller and more aware of consumption, they are looking for objects that play multiple roles."

"I'm an incredibly curious person, so I'm always thinking of new ideas, even if it's to my detriment. I think it helps to surround yourself with creative people. My partner is creative and my friends are all different types of creative people, from writers to printmakers. It helps me to get out of my bubble and think about something different."

important to my process. Before, I had only thought about experimentation as a fun part that I sometimes have time for, rather than something that I need. With this realization, I want to give it more value—which is difficult, because it doesn't always pay the bills."

Natalie's Edinburgh studio is provided by Workshop and Artists Studio Provision Scotland (Wasps), a charity that offers affordable studio space for creatives in 20 buildings across Scotland. In her studio, she has a Skutt kiln named "Gloria," a large work table, a drying cabinet, shelves for storing her moulds and a room for storing stock and packing orders. As Scotland is cold and humid, she finds a dehumidifier to be particularly useful when drying out her moulds. She shares her studio space with two other people, which increases the financial stability of her business: "Ceramics comes with a lot of equipment, and not everyone can afford that when starting out. So sharing my studio allows me to cover certain costs whilst making ceramic equipment available to others." In addition to selling her work to various stockists and online through platforms such as Etsy, Natalie also teaches workshops.

Inspired by the "warm, minimal feeling" of Hornsea Pottery's forms, Natalie runs a varied practice that is driven by a desire to make timeless, functional pieces that bring beauty to the everyday. In addition to her functional pottery, she also makes jewellery, affectionately known as "Nice Blobs." She started making these pieces as a way to use up the small amounts of slip that were left over from colour testing. Natalie originally thought she would specialize in jewellery, and her Nice Blobs line enables her to combine both her love of jewellery and ceramics, while also allowing her to work small and make something different each time. This combination of a minimal aesthetic within a varied practice has also led to collaborations with Ohh Deer, Savannah Storm and Scottish illustrator Maria Storian. Natalie knew Maria before they collaborated, and she asked Maria if she wanted to try transferring her drawings from paper to clay. Natalie had wanted to experiment with her work as a blank canvas, to see how it could be used by others in creative ways in order to reach new audiences and highlight the flexibility of ceramics as a medium. The two continue to collaborate, and in 2019 presented *Awrite Hen*, an exhibition in which they "played with imagery of women and chickens."

While her work can best be described as serenely minimal, her practice is exciting and varied, with many more interesting projects and avenues of experimentation on the horizon. "I define success by creating a sustainable practice for myself where I can develop new work and also have time away from my practice without worrying," Natalie says. ✽

"I enjoy the science involved in precision."

nataliejwood.com
@nataliejwooddesigns

PARIAN AND ITS HISTORY

At the suggestion of one of her tutors, Simon Ward, Natalie started using parian (a porcelain) in the final year of her studies at Gray's School of Art. She had wanted to colour her clay body. "I love parian, as it's so white and it takes colour very well, allowing me to really be creative in my use of colour," Natalie says.

Parian is one of four bodies, or "pastes," used by 18th and 19th century British porcelain manufacturers: hard paste porcelain, soft paste porcelain, bone china and parian. It was named after the Greek island of Paros, which is renowned for its parian marble—parian ware was designed to imitate carved marble statuary and thus is sometimes referred to as "statuary porcelain."

There is some debate as to which Stoke-on-Trent company developed the paste, with credit either going to the Copeland & Garrett factory, sometime between 1842 and 1844, or Mintons in 1845. It was designed as a casting slip, can achieve sharp modelling, takes colour well and has a vitrified surface that does not require glazing. As with all clay bodies, there are some drawbacks: "I've used parian clay for a while now so I'm used to its little quirks and I consider them when making new work," Natalie says. "I can't stack parian work in the kiln because it leaves flash marks and I can't make work with open sides because it has a tendency to warp. Little things like those can really dictate what forms I take forward to production." Regardless, the ware's saturated colours and crisp lines complement Natalie's minimal aesthetic.

MEMORY AND THE LANDSCAPE OF TIME

INGRID WENS

Writer, historian and activist Rebecca Solnit writes in her 2006 essay "The Ruins of Memory" that "Memory is always incomplete, always imperfect, always falling into ruin; but the ruins themselves, like other traces, are treasures: our links to what came before, our guide to situating ourselves in a landscape of time." When Solnit's words are considered alongside the wares of Dutch ceramist Ingrid Wens, her plates and platters can be understood as evocative physical manifestations of the invisible, layered and obscured aspects of memory.

Ingrid grew up in a small village in the Netherlands situated close to the Belgium border, in a home in which she was encouraged to be creative and active. After studying mainly two-dimensional art at the art academy in Tilburg, Netherlands, she took up teaching secondary school art, which, in addition to her ceramics practice, she continues to do one or two days a week. Initially, Ingrid was drawn to ceramics as a way to work more three dimensionally. At first, she tried to find a woodworking shop but instead found ceramics courses on offer only a few minutes bike ride away. What caught her interest with ceramics, Ingrid says, was the challenge of finding "a balance between functionality and aesthetics." When she came to the decision to "take ceramics on more seriously," she enrolled at the Arendonk Academy in Belgium. "Belgium has a very extensive adult education system, which for me was such a special time of my life," she says. "Just to be able to go through a second extensive learning period has brought me so much joy and knowledge."

"Clay tends to reveal its possibilities over time. I don't think I'll ever get bored with it."

"I like the challenge of finding a balance between functionality and aesthetics; that's what caught my interest. I hope to become more courageous in the future, though, and move more towards aesthetics than function."

Most of Ingrid's works are sold online through Etsy and Instagram. Her studio is located on the ground floor in a former orphanage, across the street from her apartment in the centre of Tilburg. It is equipped with her favourite tool—a slab roller—as well as a large working table, electric kiln, ample storage shelves and a door to the garden, which can be opened up on nice days. "I don't produce a lot, and rather take my time for the objects that leave my studio," she says. "In general, they all have their own unique look. I do use moulds, but it's never my goal to make identical platters. They all get their own look through colouring, glazing and decorating." Her mornings are often spent working on her laptop and planning lessons. After lunch, she heads over to the studio—planning her work schedule and drying times in advance—then closes the day by initiating an overnight firing, if one is needed.

For the most part, Ingrid makes plates and platters. "They're the objects with which I can express myself best," she says. "I love throwing, but it just doesn't come as naturally to me as working with slabs, probably because in the end I'm a 2D artist." A new design for a plate or platter begins by sourcing a historical image of a plate, which Ingrid then turns into a wooden mould made with the help of a rented laser cutter. The first stages of making a plate are her favourite: making slabs, using the moulds and painting, texturing and burnishing the slabs. Decorating is especially fun, she says, when she is working on new designs. Loading the kiln "can be a bit nerve-wracking, but unloading the kiln can be so satisfactory (or disappointing), especially after a glaze or luster firing."

Ceramics are a cultural archive, a form of collective memory, and Ingrid's design and approach to decoration tap into this inherent function. Her approach to surface decoration, she says, shows her "love for historical tableware, but also my curiosity in using

and combining different techniques, traditional and contemporary." By strategically removing just enough detail from 18th and 19th century plate designs, Ingrid allows her plates to still exude an essential "plateness"—historical, yet contemporary. In combination with a less-is-more approach to historical decoration, Ingrid's method creates a sense of the familiar but not the exact, like a memory in which you remember the key points but not all the minute details. The dramatic drips that are a feature of many of her plates are, in terms of gesture, minimal and controlled; they are another layer invoking ruin, the incomplete, time and trace. Ingrid explains: "Layering is important for me, as is the combination of relief, colour, and matte and glossy parts." Memory is layered and obscure but still full of so many details, and Ingrid's wares are much the same. ❊

"I love all the little 'mistakes' of old pottery: tiny pinholes, a bit of warping, small damages made by a kiln prop, and all the colours of old 'whites'—the old white tiles with the different colours given by the rest of the kiln load. Those flaws show us the people behind the tableware—the makers and the ones who used it. Industrialization made us lose contact with the origin of objects and paved the way for mass-consumption. Fortunately a counter-movement has started and handmade is valued again."

INGRID WENS

CONTEMPORARY HISTORICAL

While Ingrid's plates oscillate between the contemporary and the historical, her source material is strictly historical, yet made accessible in a contemporary, virtual way. The Rijksmuseum in Amsterdam hosts Rijksstudio, a digital archive of over 125,000 works. The high-resolution, copyright-free images can be downloaded for free, and the museum encourages people to use them in creative ways. Ingrid has taken up the call and uses the images as foundational source material for her moulds. "Once I find an interesting photo, I download it and start editing," she says. "The goal is to adjust it in a way that makes it suitable for creating a mould for a good-looking plate. The amount of editing differs per mould and sometimes I combine elements from several designs. A lot of designs don't make the cut."

rijksmuseum.nl

"Although it's not my main goal, I try to show the structure of Delft blue plates in my work, and a lot of my current moulds are based on historical plates made available by the Rijksmuseum, the Dutch national museum. They encourage designers to use their extensive image library for new designs. I edit these photos and convert them into moulds."

ingridwens.nl
@ingrid.wens.ceramics

WILD MATERIAL AND PROCESS

NATHAN WILLEVER

From his studio in Philadelphia, Pennsylvania, Nate Willever creates pots that are all about process, right down to their "wild" materials. "I make pottery because I love the process of its creation," he says. "I use dark stoneware clays with layered slips and glazes to achieve a surface that has a deep, atmospheric quality." While his pots might be minimally decorated, they exude an immense, active presence due to Nate's experimental use of natural materials and his process-focused approach to surface and form.

Material experimentation, research and testing are fundamental to Nate's process. "I am always experimenting with surfaces and forms," he says. "In the past few years I have been using local materials as clay, slips and glazes. This allows me to experiment with new surfaces often. I will crush different types of rock and blend them with my existing supply of local materials to create new surfaces." Nate hand-digs and processes his own clay. Sometimes these materials need additional processing, which gives him the opportunity to use his favourite tool, a jaw crusher. This machine crushes down rock so that it can be further processed, if needed, by a ball mill or clay mixer.

In 2018, Nate began sourcing a high iron stoneware clay from the sand mine and soil blending company Stancills, in Perryville, Maryland. He mixes this material into a cone six clay body, and the result, he says, "is a dense stoneware body that is full of character due to the impure nature of the Stancills clay." Nate explains that, for example, when the iron-rich clay is wood fired, it obtains a Japanese Bizen-like surface, and when it is reduction-fired, firefly-like spots are produced. In this way, by wilding his materials,

"Oftentimes my pots are bought by other potters, or people who have studied art. My work is often related to the history of ceramics, and people who have knowledge of ceramics often appreciate my work."

Nate connects his work to place and to ceramics history. "Using these unprocessed, wild materials has influenced how I make pots. It has produced surfaces that will age and develop over time, much like the pots from Korea, Japan and Europe that I have found inspiration in for years. My hope is that the pots show where they come from while being influenced by traditions from many cultures."

In addition to his intense interest in material, process has also played an important role in Nate's ceramic journey. His mother was an antiques dealer, and Nate grew up in a house full of old things, which he credits for fostering his appreciation for historical ceramics. He originally started potting in high school when he found himself generally disinterested in secondary school work. "I took a hand-building class and liked it, then signed up for a wheel throwing class and was quickly hooked," he recalls. "The intense concentration that is required while using the wheel in particular is what initially caught my interest." He went on to study ceramics at the Maine College of Art and Haystack Mountain School of Crafts in Deer Isle, Maine.

Nate generally works in runs of 10 to 20 pots, and he often starts with an idea for the surface: "I am either looking at a surface from a historical pot or using a surface made from a local material. The process of making is what informs new shapes. Usually, I will start to play around with either the surface by cutting with a tool, or making clay additions, or by elongating or widening the form. Small changes can make a huge impact on the finished pot." Needless to say, he finds throwing, trimming and applying slip to the work to be particularly satisfying: "These are all very immediate processes that each leave their own character to the work, if you let them. Trimming pots in particular is my favourite, as you can drastically affect the architecture of the form with trimming. There's nothing

"I believe that using handmade pottery can enrich the life of the user by connecting them to the maker. The pots I use in my home are made by my friends and colleagues whose work I admire. Each day I can choose a different pot, depending on my mood or who I want to have a 'conversation' with. This 'conversation' or connection with the maker is what I believe makes handmade objects like pots special."

more satisfying than catching the pot at the right time for trimming!" Nate either wood or gas fires with reduction atmospheres, adding an additional level of wildness and chance to his wares.

American potter Mark Hewitt eloquently described wood firing in a 2017 *Ceramics Monthly* article as "dusted by chance and painted by atmospheric turbulence … We take the earth. We light a fire. We make beauty." Nate's work and process can be described in much the same way. While his pots might at first glance appear minimal and refined, they balance this cool feeling with a sense of the monumental and the wild. His aesthetic is informed by a love of history, historical ceramics, different cultures and old objects, which works in combination with his process and materials: surfaces inform the forms, material choices influence the surfaces, and history frames it all. "I think of my work as refined, but not 'tight,'" he says. "I try to make work that fits into the contemporary way of thinking—working to make pots from a variety of influences, bringing them together and making something my own. My pots are complete when they are in service, bringing a sense of human connection to the user." ❋

"I always want to show off the clay, even if I cover it with a glaze."

THE CLAY STUDIO

Nate is currently in his third year as a resident artist at The Clay Studio in Philadelphia. The Clay Studio was founded in 1974 by five artists who needed workspace, and as an intermediary step for new ceramic graduates in need of affordable studio space and access to equipment. Within a few short years, it expanded its mandate to also include community engagement and education, and today, as stated on its website, it is "renowned for its unique ability to serve all levels of students while broadening ceramics as a contemporary art form." The residency can last for up to five years and provides a personal studio space and access to four electric kilns, two gas kilns, a glaze lab, and teaching and exhibition opportunities. Nate's studio is equipped with a wheel, pug mill and rock crusher.

nathanwillever.com
@natewillever

A MODERN TAKE ON MORRIS

PIGEON TOE CERAMICS

You might find it surprising that the Victorian designer, craftsperson and poet William Morris—best known for his complex, gothic-inspired all over textile and wallpaper designs—is mentioned in a section of this book dedicated to a minimal aesthetic. However, the British design reformer's championing of handmade and well-designed objects over poorly designed, mass-manufactured goods made under deplorable conditions has had a lasting impact on craft and ceramics. He also championed the notion of accessible, beautiful objects for everyday use, when in 1877 he said: "I do not want art for a few, any more than education for a few, or freedom for a few." While the minimal aesthetic of Lisa Jones, founder and

"The only thing that is not imitate-able or reproducible is my own unique vision. Designing for a trend or someone else is a quick path to failure. If I don't like it, why would anyone else?"

–Lisa Jones

director of Pigeon Toe Ceramics, is far from Morris' exuberance, her approach to design, business and the handmade gives new meaning to Morris' famous 1880 quote: "Have nothing in your houses that you do not know to be useful, or believe to be beautiful." In fact, in light of Lisa's paired-down slip cast aesthetic and practice, a sense of less is more in relation to use and the beautiful makes Morris' dictums relevant to minimalism as well.

Lisa considers herself a multidisciplinary "professional dabbler" with "an aversion to the excess of mass-produced goods." She founded Pigeon Toe Ceramics in 2008 in Portland, Oregon, after exploring clay as a hobby in her early twenties. In 2014, her younger sister, Samantha Hough, left a corporate job and joined her sister at Pigeon Toe. Today, this female- and sibling-powered brand takes a playful and interdisciplinary approach to craft and minimalism, selling directly to consumers, restaurants, designers and architects. They aim for "a new perspective on the beauty inherent in every day."

The business occupies a 7,000-square-foot former railroad building just off the waterfront in Portland's warehouse district, with small areas devoted to hand-building, slab work and throwing. A significant amount of space is dedicated to slip casting, as this is the business' primary means of production, but they also incorporate woven components into their work. The studio has six electric Skutt kilns and a ram press. Pigeon Toe strategically offers a broad range of objects at a variety of price ranges so that customers at various stages of life and levels of income can purchase their wares: art, design and craft are not just for the few. In addition to Pigeon Toe Ceramics, Lisa teaches creative entrepreneurship in the MFA Applied Craft and Design program at Pacific Northwest College of Art in Portland.

The majority of Lisa's designs are functional. "I love the problem solving that goes into design for everyday use," she says. "The growth of my functional line has allowed me to explore more sculptural, one-of-a-kind work that typically ends up in commercial spaces or private collections. I love not having to choose. My business supports the growth of my work and the growth of my work supports my business." Before Lisa even begins to draw a new design, she first identifies what is missing from Pigeon Toe's line or in the market itself. Then she throws numerous iterations of a prototype on the wheel or has them 3D printed. While in the design phase, she also takes into account the physicality involved in making and firing the final object, and researches if it can be made for a competitive price. If any issues arise, Lisa problem

"I don't want work in my line that is too precious to use, and to use well."

"My work is grounded in ceramics, but I also love weaving, textiles, metal work—basically anything manipulable and organic. I continue to look for ways to integrate disparate materials in a new and playful way."

solves and asks, "How do we change it to make it easier to produce? Does that change compromise the integrity of the object itself?"

Pigeon Toe's aesthetic is a contemporary, playful twist on minimalism, an aesthetic that is best illustrated in their jewellery-like lighting. Coloured slip is cast, then demoulded, shaped and cut, buffed and sanded, fired and finally assembled by hand. There is an unfolding visual, geometric rhythm to these pieces of home jewellery, as cast spheres and cones are paired with playful iterations of the saucer form. Delighting the eye and begging to be touched, the matte, light-eating surfaces of the bare ceramic parts contrast with the light-reflecting brass components, creating an object that is both useful and beautiful. Once you see one of these simple yet elegant designs, how can a mass-produced light fixture even compare? These are useful and beautiful objects for the home; Morris would approve. ✱

"One of the things we do that very few other clay companies do is tint our clay body with pigment, instead of applying it with glaze. This allows for the signature matte exterior finish in an array of tones, with the glossy glazed interior. Formulating a new colour is one of my favourite tasks, and brings in some of my previous experience as a painter, mixing colours."

"Pigeon Toe was founded with a vision to create uniquely beautiful objects grounded in American crafts and manufacturing."

pigeontoeceramics.com
@pigeon_toe

DOMESTIC MANUFACTURING

When Lisa first started her company, Etsy was still in its infancy, the 2008 recession was happening and handmade ceramics were not as popular as they are today. She believes the recession created a collective desire to make with one's own hands and support local businesses, which has contributed to Pigeon Toe's success. The company now occupies a 7,000-square-foot building and has employed as many as seven people at a time. All products are made on site. "Relying on outside manufacturing can be cost-prohibitive," Lisa says. "We make work when it's needed and desired, not to just meet an order minimum." Pigeon Toe has a robust global wholesale program and they sell directly to the consumer through their online shop.

"As we've moved into more efficient production methods, we've seen how we can sustain and grow our company. We've actually decided it's better to be a bit smaller and wear more hats. Not only does it give us more control of the day-to-day, but it also allows us to pivot quickly in response to market changes," Lisa says. Although her staff generally covers the production of Pigeon Toe's main line while she concentrates on new development and the sales side of the company, Lisa can do any of the tasks involved with the business and is able to step in when someone calls in sick or a situation arises that calls for all hands on deck.

MORE IS MORE

WRITTEN BY JULIA KRUEGER

LYDIA JOHNSON

A PAINTERLY APPROACH

ZUZKA VACLAVIK

Zuzka Vaclavik was born in Virginia but has lived in Germany, Cambodia, Florida, Minnesota, Texas and now Athens, Georgia. "During these transitory moments in my life, making art was already a passion and grounding force for me," she says. As a child, she took weekend drawing lessons from a Czech painter and studied art at the Universities of Texas and Georgia. Although she has been painting and doing other forms of art throughout her life, she only turned to ceramics around three years ago, taking a community ceramics course to shake things up. "I really wanted to be a beginner at something again, to have that feeling one has as a beginner—learning new skills, the freedom to explore and not being quite as serious with yourself." She has since brought to the field of ceramics a brave and sophisticated approach to surface and form that is rooted in her background as a painter and is bolstered by her fearless approach to failure and embracing of experimentation.

Zuzka approaches the three-dimensional forms of her pots as she would a two-dimensional canvas, emphasizing gesture and intuition—with active slashing line and sgraffito work, bold fields of colour and confident strokes of glaze, slip and lustre. However, unlike the surfaces of a painting, which she is accustomed to reworking, once the glaze is fired, manipulating the surface of her ceramics becomes much more difficult. Zuzka does not let this stop her, however, and often sandblasts, reglazes and refires her wares. "I want to see how far I can take it," she says. "I want my surface work to enhance the form and not take away from it." Atmospheric firings are her favourite; she describes the process as magical and unpredictable.

"Art is work. I don't consider this a bad thing. Creation is a serious form of play. Pushing my limits in the studio and learning new ways of doing things keeps me inspired and motivated."

"The physicality and muddiness of the material spoke to me: it was wet, sloppy and fun."

When she does an electric firing, she improvises and experiments to try to obtain a similar effect to that of an atmospheric firing.

Experimentation and improvisation, however, often bring failures—and Zuzka unashamedly describes her failure rate as high. "At demos of more seasoned potters, who make the process seem so easy, I want to say, That's not it! Show the other parts, show the collapse, show the struggle!" Zuzka says. "Sometimes I see the humour in it and other times I get very frustrated, but I just keep going. Regardless of how difficult a process may be or how many times a pot collapses, I believe that eventually I'll figure it out and it will be worth it." When she starts a piece, Zuzka often uses a sketchbook to work out her initial idea. However, she is more interested in experimenting with where her process will take her than sticking to her original idea. Her process is a constant negotiation between what has happened before and what is to come, and she does not let failure stop her.

"I am mainly making pots, but I do consider them to be a blend of functional objects, sculpture and painting. One interesting aspect of functional objects is that the forms have been used by people for centuries and we have an innate relationship to them. The more I make pottery, the less distinction I see between various categories and qualifiers of art."

Her painterly attention to surface and her investigative manipulations are playful and experimental, something she considers integral to her process. "I don't consider conventions and expectations when I make work, which is why I have so many different types of ceramics and paintings in my studios," she says. "I do realize that it is advantageous from a business and marketing perspective to narrow the scope of my work, as it may be perceived as not being deeply involved in any one idea, but in reality I am deeply involved in multiple ideas. I admire those artists who are able to find that one thing they want to devote their lives to. One of the things I am working on currently is imposing restraints on the amount of experimentation I have in my work, because those limitations can be freeing in a different way." ✽

"I allow myself complete freedom to brainstorm ideas within my sketchbooks. They are full of drawings and watercolours of pottery, or objects I find interesting. It may be years before I return to a certain sketchbook and use some of the ideas from it, or I might be working out an idea right away."

zuzkavaclavik.com
@ceramicsvaclavik

AN ARTIST COLONY

Zuzka has two studios: one dedicated to painting and one to ceramics. She spends five days a week at either one of them, and if she is really in the "mood to burn the midnight oil," she will spend six hours in one and then move to the other in a single day. Two days a week she also works as a dental hygienist. The ceramics studio is located in a two-car garage, and she shares this space with fellow ceramist and mentor Kyle Jones. Pastel artist Annie Morgan occupies a space above the garage. They jokingly call this space their own little artist colony, as each of them brings different strengths to the table. Kyle and Zuzka also formed a custom tile company called Tile Juice. While they are currently focused on creating their own personal work, they are available to also make tiles upon request. The ceramics studio is equipped with an electric and kick wheel, an air compressor and a sandblaster. Zuzka jokes, "I never thought I would be this excited about buying an air compressor, a piece of equipment not on my radar before ceramics."

SLOWING DOWN, EVEN WHEN YOU ARE BUSY

ASHLEY KIM

"The world of ceramics has been explained in a binary fashion—functional or sculptural. However, I see my work somewhere in between or oscillating between these two ends of the spectrum."

Domestic functional pottery is the focus of Ashley Kim's practice, but her hand-built objects play with the stereotypical vessel forms found within the home as she brings a sense of the uncanny to the table. Like her layered life as a teacher, nurse and potter, Ashley's pots are overlaid with balanced explorations of colour, texture and pattern. Although both her life and her pots could be described as layered and full, the motivation behind her work is to slow down: "My work is intended to be used in an intimate setting, namely our homes, to elevate and enrich our daily experiences of cooking, serving and eating."

Ashley came to clay in search of a creative outlet. At the time, she was working as a registered nurse and signed up for a pottery class at the Joslyn Center in Torrance, California. "I was immediately attracted to the alluring qualities of clay and saw its potentials as an expressive medium," she recalls. "After this initial exposure to the material and taking some art classes at El Camino College, I decided to fold my nursing career and return to school full time to study ceramics." She went on to study at Utah State University and Indiana University, and completed a one-month residency in Jingdezhen, China. After moving around for several years, she needed a change of pace and settled in San Diego, California.

Change is a slow but welcome process for Ashley. It can be organic, spurred on by a new tool which then leads to a fresh surface design, or it can be more purposeful. The introduction of decals to her repertoire is one such example of slow, purposeful change, as there is a collecting aspect to it. "I have compiled decal images over the last four to five years of gardening tools

and fruits and vegetables, to realize this idea of promoting gardening, slow cooking and eating—almost impossible at the pace we live at many days—and understanding where our food comes from," Ashley says. She hand-builds her vessels in cyclical, small series or batches: two to three months of making, decorating, firing and decaling. The process is then repeated, with lessons learned and changes put into place. "To me, my creative process is not much different from that of life in seasons."

Ashley has been told that she dresses like her pots, and this makes sense, as she approaches decorating her wares as if dressing them: layers of bright colours, polka dots, lines, lace textures and patterns. "In this sense, I see my work as figurative," she says. Her forms are constructed with coils and slabs, and she explains that this way of working brings subtlety and complexity to her work. Her vases, cups and baskets are uncanny, strange and mysterious, yet familiar at the same time. They are invented forms, informed by function in a way that is not stereotypical, with multiple

"Thoughtfully made functional pottery has the potential to enrich and elevate our daily domestic experience."

openings, protrusions and textures applied through a variety of means, including lace and textured rolling pins. In addition to lace, Ashley has for several years used vintage ceramics and disposable commercial plastic packaging as master mould shapes for her plaster drape moulds, adding to their sense of familiarity: "I find this way of appropriating these otherwise unwanted, neglected or wasted forms into contemporary functional forms quite noble, and it is my way of preserving the environment through reuse and recycling while at the same time highlighting our over-consuming and over-packaging tendencies."

With her multiple roles, Ashley finds that taking a break is a good way to keep inspired and motivated, because she quickly develops a craving to return to the studio. She also advises that "a good general rule of thumb is to keep making, keep working to get work out there, as people and galleries will then see, use and hopefully slow down to appreciate the work, and good food and life in general." ✻

ASHLEY KIM

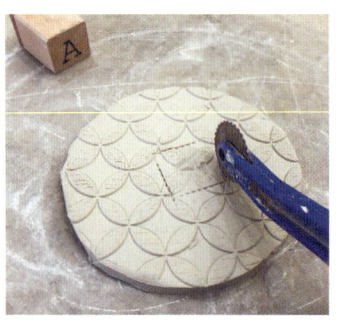

"My long-term goal is to be able to continue to make art and mature as an artist. I am back to teaching and am having to creatively juggle between teaching, nursing and studio work. This requires a lot of discipline, focus and effective time management. Although my desire is to spend more time creating, nursing and teaching ceramics make me a more rounded person and artist. So in the end, all of these activities inform who I am and what I am about."

@ashleykimclayworks

MANUAL LABOUR

Ashley's L-shaped basement home studio looks out onto her backyard in San Diego. Although she currently does not throw on the wheel, she has a Lockerbie Kick Wheel and an electric kiln in the corner near a window. She works alone and considers the 15-by-17-foot space to have ample room. She has creatively upcycled an old door into a large working table by simply attaching four legs to it. Considering that her practice currently revolves around hand-building processes, you would expect her studio to have a slab roller but that is not the case. As Ashley explains: "I enjoy rolling slabs manually a few at a time. To me, this sets the beginning of the creative process, and the slow, methodical way of rolling, pinching and coiling suits me really well for what I make."

PLEASING PATTERNS

LYDIA JOHNSON

Ceramist Lydia Johnson, from Manchester, Connecticut, considers herself a reserved person but describes her work as colourful, eclectic, assured, playful and distinctive, a product of her lively internal life rather than her quiet, outward personality. Her functional vessels are adorned—both inside and out, and from top to bottom—with joyfully bright pattern work, akin to wrapping textiles around intimate domestic forms. Her embracing of and bold, exuberant use of an all-over pattern aesthetic creates precious, sensually pleasurable functional objects for the home.

Lydia describes her work as image-based because her designs centre around how to feature the patterns. She also pushes the limits of the material by seeing how thin she can construct her wares. "I build very thin because I like the idea of a functional object being paper-thin, as if it were paper," she says. "It's almost too thin to use. The thinness transforms my work to a place that does not read like clay. It is often confused for metal or glass." Constructing such thin work requires skill, and Lydia honed hers while studying at Messiah College in Pennsylvania and Alfred University in New York. While her current body of work is hand-built, her first ceramics class was a demanding wheel throwing course, where she poured all of her efforts into making on a strict schedule, learning and experimenting.

Today, Lydia operates her business out of a 700-square-foot studio in The Armory building in Manchester and typically works there every weekday from 8 am to 5 pm. Sometimes she employs the help of an assistant, and uses a planner to schedule her tasks for the entire week, which has helped to ease

"At the beginning of my journey, I saw from a practical standpoint that I could sell functional work. Even though my interest started with a very pragmatic approach, I have been able to experience incredible freedom and creativity within the genre of functional objects."

the stress surrounding deadlines. Her studio consists of several large wooden work tables on caster wheels that her father built, a slab roller and an electric kiln. Her computer is also an indispensable tool, as she spends a considerable amount of time on it for photography, emailing and website work, and for designing her patterns and products.

Like with the Pattern and Decoration movement of the 1970s, Lydia finds inspiration in decorative traditions from around the globe: "I look at Japanese kimonos, Indian chintz fabric, high fashion runway outfits, American folk quilts, Islamic tile work, fine art, interior design and stained glass, just to name a few. Pinterest is a never-ending visual resource and I use it almost daily to discover new things. I am in awe of human creativity." She sketches her ideas numerous times both on paper and in Adobe Illustrator before ever realizing them in clay. After designing an object on the computer, she prints it to scale on paper. "This approach allows me to figure out the scale and pace of the pattern and how it's all working together

with each form," she explains. "There is so much work that goes into preparing my materials to print in clay that I don't move to the making stage until I feel I have things right in my initial design stage."

Once the design stage is complete, Lydia prints the surface pattern using stencils onto both sides of a slab of clay. Her work is often mistaken for nerikomi, a Japanese process in which different coloured clays are stacked together and then sliced through to reveal unique pattern designs—Lydia's designs, on the other hand, are printed onto the clay's surface. Then through the strategic use of moulds, and by cutting, darting and folding the clay (a process inspired by the construction of clothing), Lydia transforms her two-dimensional slabs into three-dimensional objects. "All my forms can be unfolded into rectangles or circles," she explains. "Because of this approach, there is a particular, elemental nature to my repertoire of forms." Above all else, her work is both a pleasure to look at and a sensual treat to use. ✴

"When working with a new form, it's better to make a few pieces start to finish rather than producing a full kiln load right off the bat. I have a tendency to go all-in early on with a new idea and take risks and hope for the best, which isn't always the smartest approach. Clay has taught me to be methodical, patient and persistent."

"My aesthetic is colourful and eclectic. I think my aesthetic is informed more so by my rich internal life rather than my outward personality. I consider myself to be reserved, which my work is not. I can be warm, playful and sensitive, yet also quite intense and serious. I suppose I see those qualities in my work."

LYDIA JOHNSON

"I enjoy the moment between the initial design stage and the actualization of those designs in clay, especially the very first time a design is created in clay."

LOOKING AT THE NUMBERS

Lydia considers her business to be sustainable, as she is able to support herself through sales and workshops. She teaches workshops out of her studio and only travels once or twice a year to give presentations. She sells her work directly to her customers through her website and at events throughout the year. Galleries and retailers also carry Lydia's work, often finding her through Instagram, highlighting the importance of being active on social media. "You have to be incredibly disciplined, focused and driven," Lydia advises regarding running a business. "You also have to have tunnel vision, set goals and be able to fight through the low points. Most importantly, you have to be willing to look at the numbers. As they say, the numbers do not lie. Your heart can deceive you. I think that is the hardest battle—between your head and heart, the entrepreneur and artistic spirit. They can absolutely live in harmony, but sometimes it takes a long time to get there."

lydiajohnsonceramics.com
@lydiajohnso

AN ALIEN FLORAL VIBE

MEGAN BOGONOVICH

What would a garden on a distant alien planet look like? Would it be filled with big, bright colours and clusters of coral-like structures? Or would it evoke a dream world filled with collections of dollar store plastic flowers? Vermont-based ceramist Megan Bogonovich might very well have the answer, as she creates bright coloured porcelain sculptures with what she describes as an "alien floral vibe."

Megan always wanted to be an artist. As a child growing up in Bennington, Vermont, she remembers being "curious about anyone in town with a creative lifestyle: jewellers, rug makers, illustrators and novelists." However, she originally focused on painting and drawing, only to discover ceramics in the summer before her final year at the Maryland Institute College of Art. "Clay was an immediate fit," she recalls. "It felt intuitive and natural right away." After that initial community college summer course, Megan couldn't leave the ceramics studio and ended up studying an extra year as a continuing education student before pursuing graduate studies in Montana, "with the goals of getting my own space and being left alone to make stuff. I think 13-year-old me would be pleased." Today, she has her own small studio building on her Vermont property in the woods. It is equipped with two electric kilns, a wheel, an extruder and lots of plaster moulds.

Multiplicity and the pairing of different parts are key conceptual frameworks to Megan's practice. She usually begins with an idea for a component or part, makes a mould of it, slip casts it and then sees how the new shape interacts with the cast forms she has already made. "I think of the assembly of cast parts as

"I'm inspired by artists who seem unencumbered by the history or functional potential of the material—it's just a raw material to engage with. I like seeing loose and experimental work, work that doesn't begin with technique or a specific clay skill set."

a toy set that I can rearrange," she explains. "Knowing that I am heading towards something floral and exuberant, I solve problems and make compositional choices as I build. The component parts are the only real planning." She also works on several pieces at once, "floating between art making and manufacturing," creating a balance between improvisation and methodical organization. Although her coral-like objects are encrusted with intricate detail, the parts themselves are simple shapes, quickly formed with the aid of an extruder. Her surfaces are also covered with repeating patterns, textures and surface treatments, including china paint, oxides, lustres and decals. Each organic cluster is an otherworldly garden from the ocean floor, another world or maybe from your dreams.

Megan's current sculptures are curious, bold, colourful and busy, and follow the decorative tradition of ornamenting the home. "I'm not sure it would be the work I would be attracted to if I had not been its maker," she says. "However, the work is its own beast and I

follow along. It can't resist ornament, and I can't leave well enough alone." For Megan, this body of work relates to her previous series through the use of florals, colour and a playful sense of goofiness.

Although she lives in the woods and has a flower garden, don't mistake these floral sculptures as a manifestation of a passionate interest in the natural world. "I'm not disinterested in the natural world, but I think my primary influence is the man-made world," Megan says. "Glitzy things, wonky things, ridiculous human stuff. Nutso fashion, overindulged homeowners, the shiny new constructions and the falling apart wreckage." Considering her works are influenced by the man-made world yet are definitely floral in subject matter, they can be read as a 21st-century update of the 18th-century porcelain flowers crafted by the French royal manufactory of Vincennes and owned by historical figures such as Madame de Pompadour. However, Megan adds a subversive quality to her bouquets, as the inspiration for her flowers does not reside in the natural world but rather in the dollar store and in modern moments such as billboards interrupting a pristine landscape, or litter and lawn ornaments.

The tension between the natural and artificial, worldly and otherworldly, and luxury and the dollar store are what cultivate the "alien floral vibe" in Megan's work and make her ceramic angiosperms so imaginatively compelling. Megan says it is the pursuit of that single object that keeps her going, and in the meantime who knows what will pop up next in her porcelain garden. ✻

"Being creative is necessary for my mental health. I know that getting into the studio will comfort and invigorate me in the same way an athlete craves those endorphins."

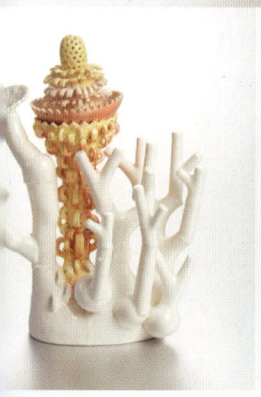

"My instinct as an artist is to work with multiple parts, many bits and pieces, organized intuitively and in relation to the qualities of the individual component. For the floral sculptures, I have created an archive of plaster moulds. The shapes, textures and forms that result from slip casting the moulds en masse provide the characters I build with. The lure of the compositional problem solving that this building method creates is a big part of what draws me into the studio. Each piece has potential for reconfiguration. A part can be manipulated, cropped and added onto, and suddenly its purpose can shift."

FROM WEDDING CAKE TOPPERS TO FLORAL SCULPTURES

Megan spent a number of lucrative years focused on creating a small production line, mainly wedding cake toppers of couples sporting human bodies and animal, robot or unicorn heads, which she sold on the Internet through platforms such as Etsy. However, the demands associated with online communication and relentless repetitive making led to burnout. "There was a window where it might have made sense to hire assistants and begin marketing and enlarging the enterprise as a coherent business," she says. "But my heart wasn't in it." She continues to sell her work daily on Etsy, as she likes to have some independence in the marketing and sales of her work, but her focus has shifted. She now teaches at a local college two days a week, spends three days a week in her studio and reserves the weekends for family. Her part-time teaching job has eased the pressure to create market-driven work, and she can now experiment and focus on making objects that take a bit more time.

meganbogonovich.com
@melabogo

ECLECTIC BOHEMIAN

SHANNON BUTLER

"I look at ceramics as problem solving in the prettiest, most interesting ways possible."

Shannon Butler's take on a bohemian aesthetic can best be described as playful, eclectic, bright and layered. Her work, whether it be functional or sculptural, is covered in bright colours and textural patterning, requiring multi-step decorative processes from start to finish. After completing her studies at Emily Carr Institute of Art and Design in Vancouver, British Columbia, and the Alberta University of the Arts in Calgary, Alberta, she returned home to Fort St. John, BC, and started her brick-and-mortar shop, kilnhouse studio, which she operated for eight years. Upon the birth of her son, Clyde, she closed up shop and moved her studio into her garage. She currently works while he naps, and holds a monthly auction of her ceramic works on Instagram.

Having grown up on a farm north of Fort St. John, Shannon is accustomed to an active and hard-working, independent, do-it-yourself lifestyle. "Definitely something about my farm roots drew me to making tangible ceramic art," she says. "Growing up on a cattle ranch, life is just very hands-on. The experience of getting in there and getting dirty was not foreign to me, when all I knew as a child was the art of constant problem solving. It built a type of confidence in me. I knew I could fix problems and build things because I'd seen my dad do it, and I was also attracted to the freedom of not having to work for someone else." Like farming, there is a cyclical, process-oriented rhythm to ceramics, with making, drying, firing, reclaiming, cleaning, selling and shipping. Shannon plans her day every morning, and then when nap time comes, she gets to work.

Typically, a piece begins with a sketch. "I use my sketchbook a lot to plan ahead, especially for what decorating decisions I will be making," Shannon says. She reworks an idea numerous times in order to figure out how to bring more to the design, making sure to follow her own natural inclinations and rhythms. What inspires her is nothing short of an eclectic cacophony of textures, forms and pop culture. Everything from a crochet pillowcase to the embroidered daisies found on an inside pocket of a pair of jeans, to a buttercup on the ground, a statue of the Virgin Mary, vintage wallpaper or a weathered farmer smoking a cigarette in his field—all, in some form or another, make it into her work. For example, she was recently inspired by the memory of a tame milk cow she had as a child: "I thought about how underappreciated cows really are, so I wondered how I could celebrate this creature with my design. I started to add more elements of whimsy to my drawing, such as a cowbell with a large leather collar that had embroidered roses on it, and then I thought of line quality and how I could carve to several different depths and widths so the relief design would have lots of interest."

Balance and texture play an important role in Shannon's design decisions, a lesson she learned while studying under Katrina Chaytor in Calgary, who encouraged her to approach surface decoration like considering what to wear in the morning. Consequently, Shannon has been told that she looks a lot like her pots. "In my work, I try to mix textures to give visual interest," she says. "I try to do this by juxtaposing matte surfaces alongside glazed ones, kind of like how I would mix a very feminine floral top with a utilitarian pair of jeans and boots to balance the look, and I think I look at decorating pots that way, too."

Katrina also introduced Shannon to the usefulness of plaster within the studio. Shannon obtains her ornately all-over textured surfaces by carving the designs from her sketchbook into a plaster tablet—a useful hint from Shannon is that thrift store lasagna pans are perfect vessels for pouring those plaster tablets. Once the tablet is carved, a slab of clay is rolled

"I believe my business is sustainable as long as I keep producing work that's authentic to my life experience and find an audience for it. My plan is to never stop creating until the day I die."

SHANNON BUTLER

onto it so that the clay picks up the design, creating a raised line drawing. The textured clay slabs are then fashioned by hand into various shapes. For Shannon, mugs are wonderful utilitarian objects, as they serve as canvases for her designs, which in turn have an intimate connection with the user because their surfaces and textures are touched by hands and lips.

In addition to her best-selling bohemian textured mugs, Shannon creates ceramic and mixed-media sculptures that are replete with layered patterns. "Both fortunately and unfortunately, there really isn't anything in ceramics that I'm *not* interested in, and I like to switch between genres to keep it interesting and challenging for myself," she says. Shannon has recently started sculpting animal planters, inspired by kitschy 1950s examples, which she covers in painted underglaze floral designs. Experimentations such as these keep her practice fresh and inspiring. "The ideas have never run out, but my brain does get overwhelmed with too many, at times!" she laughs. "I've made peace with the fact that some pieces won't get made or maybe it'll happen when I have more time at 85." ❖

"No doubt when you turn your art into your money maker, your relationship to your own art can change. I strive to have some balance both by making objects that are my most popular and then having times when I make 'whatever the hell I want'—and honestly, usually my audience prefers the work that's deeply inspired and came from a place of fearlessness. People are so intuitive, they can sense on a gut level if the work comes from an authentic and fresh place, and I believe they're attracted to that."

kilnhousestudio.com
@kilnhousestudio

A CREATIVE GARAGE

Shannon's layered, all-over, eclectic aesthetic is expressed on the walls of her creative studio space, as she tapes and tacks anything she likes onto them. "It's my studio so I let it run wild," she says. "I have a few plants in there, too, cleaning the air. It's really cozy and makes me realize I don't need much to create work." Her studio is in a renovated one-car garage. She insulated the garage, put up walls and replaced the solid garage door with a windowed door so that light could pour into her studio. Space heaters warm the studio during the colder months—from October to March—and hot water has to be hauled in from the house. Hauling water sometimes proves challenging, but Shannon makes the task manageable by working in small batches of seven to ten one-of-a-kind pieces. Her studio also houses a number of her favourite pieces of equipment: "I love my canvas-covered table because it's sturdy and large, giving me the freedom to create as big as I'd like, and I can't live without my wheel, banding wheel and kiln of course—all three are an integral part of the studio." Shannon has also creatively repurposed a Tim Horton's donut rack—courtesy of her sister, who owns some franchises—into a damp room. Although her studio has almost everything she needs, her kiln is not in the garage, but close by in a backyard shed, in order for her to avoid exposure to toxic fumes.

AN ABUNDANCE OF PROCESS

PATTIE CHALMERS

When describing her process, Pattie Chalmers says, "I approach my work in different ways, depending on what my intention is. Usually, I have an idea, something I imagine that I would like to see. Then I make it. I pinch and coil, and slab and slump. I throw and cast, and draw and trace. I slip and underglaze, and sgraffito and Mishima. I glaze and decal and lustre and glue. I flock and leaf and paint and polish. I mix media and stick to clay. My approach is as varied as the work looks. I don't have one way to work." Needless to say, Pattie's approach to ceramics consists of abundance—more is more in process, material, problem solving, narrative and presentation. A professor of art in Carbondale, Illinois, Pattie grew up as the middle of three sisters in Winnipeg, Manitoba, and originally studied to be a printmaker before being "seduced by the ceramic trifecta of shape, form and surface."

Pattie does not just make pots, sculptures, installations, prints or even embroideries. What kinds of work does she make? "Any. All. I try not to show favouritism," she says. Pattie describes herself as a storyteller whose works weave "a tangle of narrative possibilities." There is always more to her surfaces, vignettes and stories than first meets the eye. Onto the surfaces of her pots she applies the skills she learned as a printmaker—a craftsperson who carves and marks a printing plate's surface. Pattie adeptly combines all-over sgraffito textile-like pattern work with a cameo view into another world. The cameos are strangely familiar, as if from a long lost memory. After carefully hand-forming a vessel, Pattie covers it in a white slip, then meticulously scratches patterns through the slipped surface.

"I make the work that I want to make. I would always like to increase my audience, but I don't spend a lot of time chasing a specific audience or a particular gallery. I don't even know if that works. I am interested in trying new things and showing in new places and having conversations with new people."

326 CERAMICS

The term "horror vacui," which literally means fear of empty space, is used in art to describe the filling of an entire surface with detail, but it would be unfair to categorize Pattie's decorative style as fear-driven. Instead, her patterns serve as frames, adding layered complexity to the surface of her pots. She sources her images and patterns from four-for-a-dollar comic books, movies of the week and family photo albums. For Pattie, "connecting narrative image to object ties me to a tradition of vessel making in ceramics, and the experience is gratifying."

Not only do the family-inspired cameos serve as windows into other worlds and memories, they also evolve into sculptural ceramic figures ranging in size from a small collectible ceramic figurine to the height of a toddler. Pattie hand-builds her figures and sometimes has to fire them in multiple parts before assembling them, along with other ceramic objects and characters, into semi-fictional vignettes. Like a challenging puzzle, these vignettes foster layer upon layer of meaning for both Pattie and the viewer. While

"I make pots that express the quality of a handmade object and the tactile quality of clay."

a collection of work like *Every Day I Think of You*—Pattie's ambitious installation of 365 ceramic objects that each relate to a specific person—might appear haphazard, the arrangement of the various components is purposeful: "I make groupings of fabricated objects arranged into constellations or clusters, making associations with cabinets of curiosity or my great aunt's china cabinet. The objects themselves are specific to my remembrances but become stimulants for other memories, for both the viewers and myself, and are a ready reminder of our ability to condense such a variety of experiences into seemingly mundane mementos."

Before ever rolling out a slab, pinching a pot or painstakingly scratching into a surface, Pattie first plays around with ideas in her head and on paper. She will often remake an idea several times before it feels complete. "I read and look and talk, and I am not sure, but it seems my doing these things moves my work forward. I don't want to be bored, and I always have new things I want to do, so change is always coming. I am also always trying to get better at what I do, and I like learning new things, so that also keeps me moving." Studio life, however, is full of ups and downs, and sometimes making art can feel more like work, especially when your day is filled with tasks or packing up finished pieces. However, when busy work is involved, Pattie will listen to books on tape or music, but, as she says, "in the end, I don't mind working hard, so I don't need much to motivate me to get working." ✣

"Failure can happen at any time; if you don't learn from your mistakes, then you are destined to repeat them. I do both. Clay is a fickle partner. When things go wrong, I shake my fist in the air and say, 'Ceramics, why must you vex me?' But then I put my head down and attempt to problem solve my way out of whatever has gone wrong."

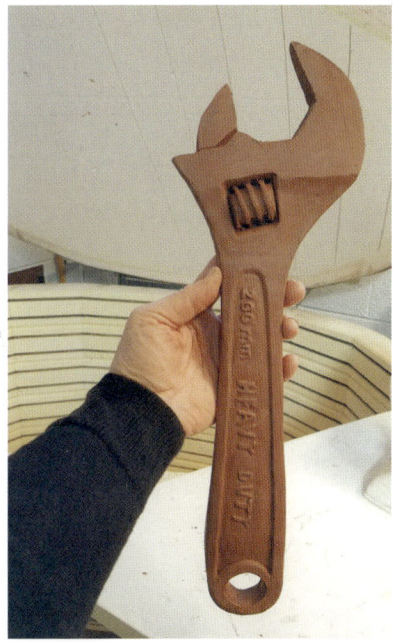

"I think a lot about what I make and why I make it. I read and look and talk, and I am not sure, but it seems my doing these things moves my work forward. I don't want to be bored, and I always have new things I want to do, so change is always coming. I am also always trying to get better at what I do, and I like learning new things, so that also keeps me moving."

pattiechalmers.com
@ladypattiechalmers

A STUDIO AT SCHOOL

For Pattie, an added benefit of teaching at Southern Illinois University in Carbondale, which she has done since 2005, is access to the university's equipment, including a community glaze room and gas and electric kilns. But her favourite tools are her hands, along with her imagination and curiosity. She is constantly seeking to learn new things, and because her studio is located at the university, students, colleagues and peers are an accessible and constant resource. Balancing all the duties of teaching and being a full-time artist can be a challenge, which means that the majority of Pattie's studio time takes place during evenings and weekends. "I spend more late nights in the studio than are probably healthy," she says. "[But] I am grateful to be part of this enriching academic setting."

PATTERN POINTS AND PLAYS

TANYA EVERARD

Tanya Everad's practice focuses on functional, well-made intimate vessels that are a pleasure to use and that enrich the eating and drinking experience. She currently creates cups, mugs, small- to medium-sized plates and small vases out of her home in her basement studio in Calgary, Alberta. While Tanya's pots adhere to the design maxim "form follows function," her complex pattern work enhances the form and highlights its function, all at the same time; perhaps for Tanya, the saying should be "form follows function, but pattern points and plays."

Tanya has always been attracted to and curious about things in the ground, which led her to pursue degrees in geological and environmental engineering and geotechnical engineering. After working and then focusing on family as a stay-at-home mom, Tanya and her family settled in Calgary in 2010. She started potting in 2014 after taking a recreational evening ceramics course at Calgary's Alberta University of the Arts. The course taught her the basics, including a brief introduction to the myriad possibilities associated with surface decoration. She continues to teach herself about ceramics by reading everything she can find on the subject: the Ceramics Art Network and Musing About Mud are two of her favourite sources online.

For the first few years of her pottery business, Tanya Everard Ceramics, Tanya only had a small test kiln, which dictated the amount and size of work she could make and fire, but she has recently procured a larger "vintage but like new" Skutt kiln, which will enable her to create larger pieces. When firing her kilns, she relies on a kitchen timer, witness cones and her accumulated knowledge on how long it takes, meaning she

"I try to make people enjoy the tranquility of eating and drinking from handmade, unique and functional works of art. The world is a busy and often troublesome place, and if I can make people feel special by holding something lovely, or to feel comfort and at peace for a short time during their busy day, then I've done something to make their life a little easier."

"My approach to ceramics is along the lines of 'it's all just a big experiment.'"

has to babysit the kiln when it is firing. Her kilns are in her garage and her secondhand wheel is in her basement studio along with a work table, sink and shelving.

"I do not consider myself to be a typical production potter, however," Tanya says, "because some of my pieces can take a considerable time to decorate, and many of my pieces are one-off or unique. My ceramic work is something I can do from home that keeps me busy when the kids are at school and is something that I am developing so I can continue to do it in retirement. I am gradually learning what it is that I like to do, and how to make it financially viable, but I don't have all the answers yet."

Although not a production potter per se, Tanya currently creates two lines or bodies of work. Her Printworks series are wheel-thrown mugs, bowls, teapots and covered vessels decorated with ceramic tissue transfers. She silkscreens some of the tissue transfers by hand in her studio while others she purchases through ceramic suppliers. Tanya uses the transfer patterns to "fill the blank porcelain surface and convey a sense of rustic comfort, warmth and simplicity." As she says, "To me, the decorations remind me of freshly washed cotton printed bed sheets or summer dresses, and maybe convey a sense of a 'simple life in the country' or an 'at home with Grandma' kind of feeling." Her Slip-Trailed series is often

hand-painted, featuring bold black lines, bright fields of repeating colour and gold lustre. They are designed to convey a sense of sophistication and elegance. "This work represents everything I feel that I am not: contrast, colourful, sweet, classy or sophisticated," Tanya says. "I like to play with colour and patterns, and I love the precision and technical challenge that comes with the creation of a two-dimensional pattern onto a three-dimensional object."

   Whenever Tanya is inspired by a pattern she sees, she transcribes a sample of it, along with colour ideas, into her sketchbook, returning to her sketchbook later for inspiration. She researches patterns from around the world, including Japanese sashiko embroidery patterns used for quilting kimonos, Marimekko designs, Islamic geometric tiling patterns, Polynesian textile and tattoo patterns, and patterns made using the Zentangle Method, a simple way to create unplanned, structured, non-representation all-over pattern work. "I consider regularly repeated geometric patterns intriguing, and form a kind of visual calculus

based on unspoken fundamental tenets," Tanya says. "Collecting, creating and displaying these patterns on everyday pottery is a continued celebration of their diversity and intellectual and artistic complexity."

Pattern and form compete cooperatively with each another in Tanya's work; there is a constant sense of organized experimentation and play. Sometimes, the decorated surface is found on the interior of a vessel, where it will inevitably be covered by food and only revealed as the meal is consumed. Other times both the top and bottom are decorated, leading one to wonder, "Which way is up?" Or perhaps it is a special surprise for someone washing dishes, revealed when the vessel is turned upside down for drying. When decorating a plate, Tanya carefully articulates each part with a contrasting pattern, which is separated by a band of gold lustre but connected by way of a common colour. This approach creates a design-based visual tension between form and surface, which in turn makes viewing and using these vessels intriguing and pleasurable. ✣

PAPER, PEN, CLAY

Although Tanya's Slip-Trailed line includes some very complicated patterns, the tools she uses to execute her pattern work are surprisingly simple and easy to find. For pattern-related inspiration, Tanya turns to the Internet, where she looks at old pattern books such as Jules Bourgoin's 1879 publication *Les eléments de l'art Arabe*. When she finds a pattern she likes, she prints it on regular printer paper to the scale she needs. She has learned that the paper expands when it gets wet, so she adjusts for this. Then, when the vessel is at the leather-hard state, she puts the paper on the surface and gently traces the pattern with a ballpoint pen, marking the clay underneath. She uses a ballpoint pen so that she can see what lines she has already traced. Once the tracing work is done, Tanya uses a Xiem Precision Applicator tool to trail the underglaze atop the patterned lines. She then paints colour between the lines using any type of fine-tipped brush—nothing fancy, just whatever works.

tanyaeverardceramics.ca
@tanyaeverard

REPAIR - REMIX - REJUVENATE - REPURPOSE

ALISON HUNTER

In Ireland, potsherds—or broken pieces of ceramic—are referred to as "chaneys," and they are found in fields and washed up on beaches. In the past, children collected chaney pottery as tokens, toys and play money. These objects are very much a part of the history of ceramics. Like the children of the past, Alison Hunter also collects chaneys in and around the coastal town of Sligo in North West Ireland, where she lives and works, and repurposes them. She combines these old, broken plate fragments with wet and needle-felted sheep's wool, and in the process she repairs, remixes, rejuvenates and repurposes something otherwise seen as broken, useless and forgotten into something new yet old, all at the same time.

Alison first came across chaneys as a child growing up on a farm, when freshly ploughed fields would reveal these miniature windows into the past. Later, she completed a degree in Irish heritage and worked in built heritage conservation. "I'm very interested in our vernacular built heritage," she says. "I love old cottages and that they were built using materials in the locality. Crockery is synonymous with these buildings." These old examples of vernacular architecture can be filled with abandoned material culture like a broken plate, which can lead to inspiration. Alison also has a diploma in textiles, and it was during these studies at St. Angela's College in Sligo that she started to combine her interest in the material culture of the past with fibre. She also had the opportunity during her fibre-based studies to work with a local pottery, Breeogue Pottery, where she honed her ceramic skills.

In addition to the chaneys, Alison also works with larger plate fragments, like ones left behind in

"I am always amazed how something as ordinary as clay and pottery can tell us so much about the past. The tiny shards that the earth gives up can tell us so much about the creation of the original vessel and how it served a valuable function such as storing grain."

abandoned sheds and cottages. She never breaks plates for her work; she only uses found pieces sourced from the environment or local flea markets, or sent to her as part of a commission. Alison painstakingly researches these ceramic fragments from the past, as she likes to know the date and more about the makers and designs associated with the chaneys. "I choose a plate and study the pattern, design and colour in detail," she explains, "asking questions like, how can the pattern be enhanced, changed by taking certain elements and exaggerating those in order to complement and respect the original design? I always draw or paint a very rough sketch so I have an idea of what I'd like."

Sometimes it is the pattern found on a chaney that serves as inspiration. For example, Alison felted an entire plate featuring a blue-and-white pouring jug with flowers around a sherd that only had two blue stripes on it. She then crafted the felted plate into a ceramic one, layering and connecting iterations and materials in an innovative and complex way. Other times, it is the shape of the plate combined with the

"Some chaneys have survived for over 100 years—although no longer whole, they are still here. These are given a longer lifetime with the combination of wool felt, and a new function from the original, with a mix of colour, pattern and texture. The process is one of care, thought and respect."

"Plates are memory triggers. They become part of people's lives and memories without them realizing it."

pattern that serves as inspiration. In one such example, she fashioned a missing, highly textured lip of a plate out of wool, creating a framing-like device, although the blue-and-white flowers creep beyond the vessel's original boundaries, adding a sense of life to an otherwise broken and somewhat useless plate.

The melting plates illustrate Alison's unique engagement with history. Time, purpose, material and fact all seem to melt and ooze together in her work. Although she takes inspiration from the found fragments, she explains that "some plates may at first offer no inspiration, but after a few months an idea starts to form and I get to work. I think there is a way to enhance any plate, even if it seems impossible. It just takes time, a lot of thought and pushing your own boundaries." Sometimes those boundaries also include what was originally there. Take "Nordic Whale," for instance, a blue-and-white plate that prominently features a blue whale. The felted part of this plate is a reimagined design that pushes the boundaries of what was into something new and wondrous. The strength of Alison's practice is that it takes history beyond facts into the realm of the possible, the imagined and the wondrous through the acts of repairing, remixing, rejuvenating and repurposing. She sees a chaney as more than just a broken object and, she says, takes "into consideration the journey it has been through, the people associated with it, the love and care given to it and the memories it made." ❋

TWO STUDIOS

Alison works out of two studios in North West Ireland. For most of the week, she works out of her home studio. "My studio is a living place of books, colour and broken ceramics, and can sometimes be quite a mess, as so much happens there," she says. "It's my creative space and it has produced a lot of work and ideas over the years." In addition to boxes of broken plates, her studio also houses her inventory of coloured wool—some of which she has dyed herself—and inspirational knick-knacks she has picked up at second-hand shops and car boot sales. Alison also shares a studio/gallery retail space with four other artists called the Weir Gallery in the town of Sligo. Her work is available for sale there, and each artist is allocated working time in the studio. For Alison, the Weir Gallery is "a great place to meet the public and to showcase my work and process."

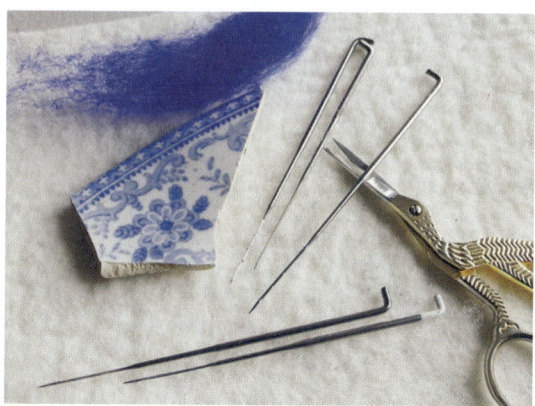

alisonhunterartist.etsy.com
@alisonhunterartist

IMPOSSIBLE OBJECTS

JANICE JAKIELSKI

The history of ceramics is filled with stories of insatiable desire and quests for knowledge. Take the story of the 18th-century Saxon elector and Polish king Augustus the Strong, who imprisoned the German alchemist Johann Friedrich Böttger in order to force him to reveal his secrets for turning base metals into gold. Böttger of course didn't hold the key to this alchemical problem, but he did discover a formula for hard-paste porcelain, which up until then was only known in China and Japan, making porcelain objects extremely valuable and rare—impossible objects, so to speak. The story of Janice Jakielski's quest for knowledge and the impossible objects she makes fits into this rich narrative of materials-based scientific and creative exploration. What unites her varied practice is an insatiable quest for material knowledge bound up in a pursuit of the limits of ceramics and what is believed to be technically possible and impossible, and through all this she creates contemporary curious and impossible objects.

At the age of 15, Janice decided she wanted to be a potter, and one Halloween even dressed up as the "Mad Potter of Biloxi," George E. Ohr. She spent numerous hours pouring over back issues of *Ceramics Monthly* that were crammed away in a closet at her high school, and for a science fair project she focused on formulating lead substitutions for glaze. She studied at Alfred University, spent time working in Japan and then attended grad school at the University of Colorado. Although Janice caught the ceramics bug early, over the course of her career she has explored glass and textiles as well. "I think that it is important to reassess goals often," she explains. "My career has

"I'm a big believer in resetting when things get uninspiring or tough. This has taken many forms over the years and I've come to realize that it really is just about entering a place of meditation to recentre and refocus. I used to throw cups a few times a year to reset; these days I play piano. As long as I'm making, it will lead me back to the studio. I spend a ridiculous amount of energy designing and building my beehives, but this always leads to a creative burst in the studio. The same thing happens with sewing, gardening or finishing up one of my many, many home projects."

taken many unexpected paths and I think if I had stubbornly stuck to what I thought was my plan I would've missed out on many opportunities."

Her quest for a new paper-thin porcelain material began in graduate school, when Janice's husband, Joshua Persky, was working as a materials engineer for a ceramic technology company. One day he brought home a sample of tape cast alumina that fascinated Janice. She immediately began experimenting with adding Elmer's glue to a clay body to see how it could increase the clay body's flexibility. Janice and Joshua eventually combined their expertise, created a company and developed a clay body formula that, unlike the highly toxic industrial versions of tape casting, is safe for application in the studio.

Janice's current body of work, which she describes as residing in the grey area between art and design, began in this place of material exploration and thinking "about function in different ways." Unlike her early forays into pottery, her current body of work is sculptural. "Cut, veneered, twirled and slotted, my vessels have a material ambiguity that brings the viewer to a place of sensory uncertainty," she says. In terms of material preparation, she begins in her Massachusetts-based home laboratory by casting coloured porcelain slurry—with the help of a tape casting machine—onto five-foot-long sheets of plastic. Once the ultra-thin casts have dried, she rolls them up for future use, as the clay body she has pioneered remains flexible for years. When she has settled on a design for one of her sculptures, she unrolls and cuts the porcelain with a vinyl or laser cutter. Then, in her "clean" workspace, which is dedicated to "assembly, design and anything not messily ceramic," she meticulously assembles the cut pieces with thin slurry and finally transfers them to a kiln shelf for firing. Generally speaking, she does not glaze her work: "I seem to gravitate to bare porcelain. I am seduced by its nakedness and the sharpness of its uncoated edges."

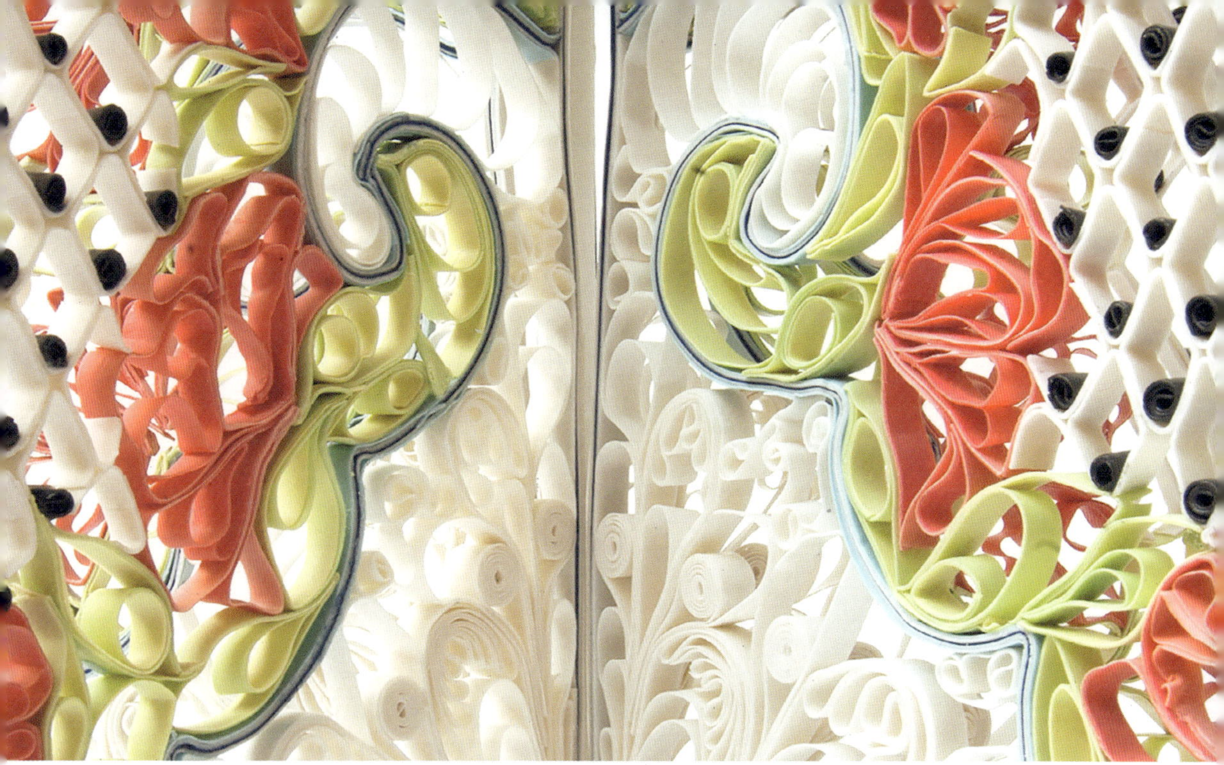

Her sculptures are inspired by historic sources and processes in order to, as she puts it, "create a moment of recognition that can then facilitate a kinship

"As a magical thinker I probably indulge a bit too heavily in escapism and I find escape in exacting craftsmanship. I continuously test the limits of my materials, pushing the boundaries of what is technically possible while still maintaining a visual connection with my audience."

"I strive to make objects that can exist in the home but are challenging enough to hold their own in more major collections."

JANICE JAKIELSKI

between viewer and object. My pieces are inspired by iconic historic vessels. I do not replicate these objects but instead re-imagine them in ways not feasible using traditional ceramic clay bodies." Before ever touching the clay, Janice meticulously translates her ideas into written descriptions, basic sketches, digital drawings and paper models or maquettes. "Much of my work is created by stacking layers of thin coloured porcelain, so I need to think carefully about how the pieces will be assembled," she explains. "It's similar to a printmaking process, starting from the bottom layer of colour and working my way to the top." She selects colours from her library of test tiles. Once all of her design options are checked and rechecked, she begins the process of cutting the porcelain.

In addition to assembling layers of porcelain into three-dimensional objects, Janice has also redefined what processes are possible in ceramics. "When I started using this thin cast porcelain I realized that all of the normal clay rules went out the window," she says. "I started to look at various paper construction

techniques because the thin, flexible sheets of porcelain act a lot like paper. I thought quilling looked pretty fun, and there is an impossible aspect in making that out of traditional clay that fascinated me." Quilling was originally practiced in Ancient Egypt, and then was used as decorative adornment in the 16th and 17th centuries in France and Italy. Like clay, which has an uncanny ability to mimic other materials, quilling, when gilded or silvered, can mimic precious metal filigree work. The layers of mimesis within her quilled works not only push the boundaries of what is possible but add conceptual depth as well.

Today, Janice alternates between teaching, residencies and her private studio practice. She also dabbles in a number of other creative pursuits, including beekeeping, which nourish her creativity. "I have found that as long as I'm making anything it will lead me back to the studio," she says. "I spend a ridiculous amount of energy designing and building my beehives, but this always leads to a creative burst in the studio." ✣

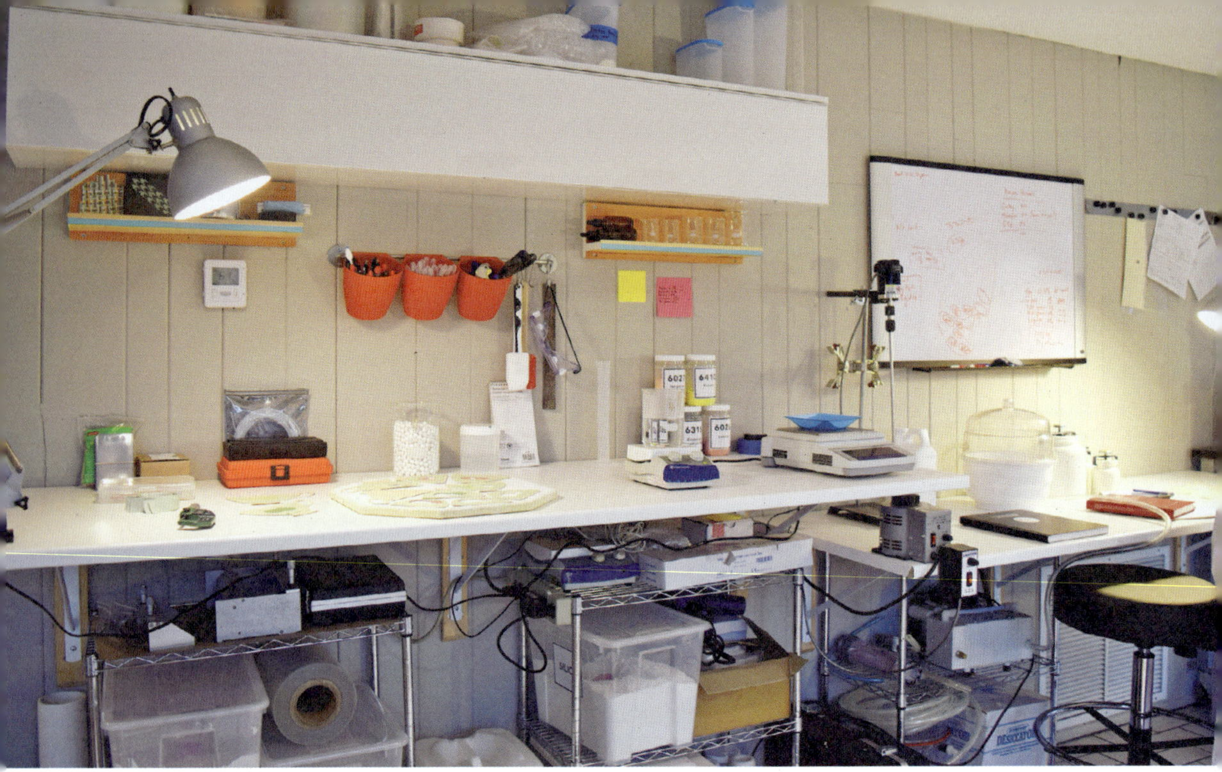

"I like to think of my studio practice as a series of mountains with a river running at the base. The mountains are the longer-term projects, the ones that I may need to set aside periodically, take a breather while climbing. The river is constantly flowing and is more playful—these are the experiments that I'm doing in the lab, the maquettes that may or may not go anywhere. For me, it's important to always have something unfinished to return to, a project that continues to lure me back into the studio."

janicejakielski.com
@janicejakielski

INDUSTRY AND SCIENCE

"I have always made do with what I have, and pride myself in being able to make work no matter the tools available, but it is amazing the difference a quality piece of machinery can make to your process," Janice says. Her favourite piece of equipment is a high shear mixer that easily mixes colourants into a consistent clay body. She shares a home studio space in Massachusetts with her husband, which they call "The Laboratory," where they do all their material experimentation and processing. Together they focus on reinventing industrial ceramic processes for studio artists, through their company, Meld Materials. Accordingly, their creative space not only contains typical ceramic equipment like a ball mill, wheel and kilns, but also includes a variety of scientific and industrial equipment, such as stir plates, a rheometer and a tape casting machine.

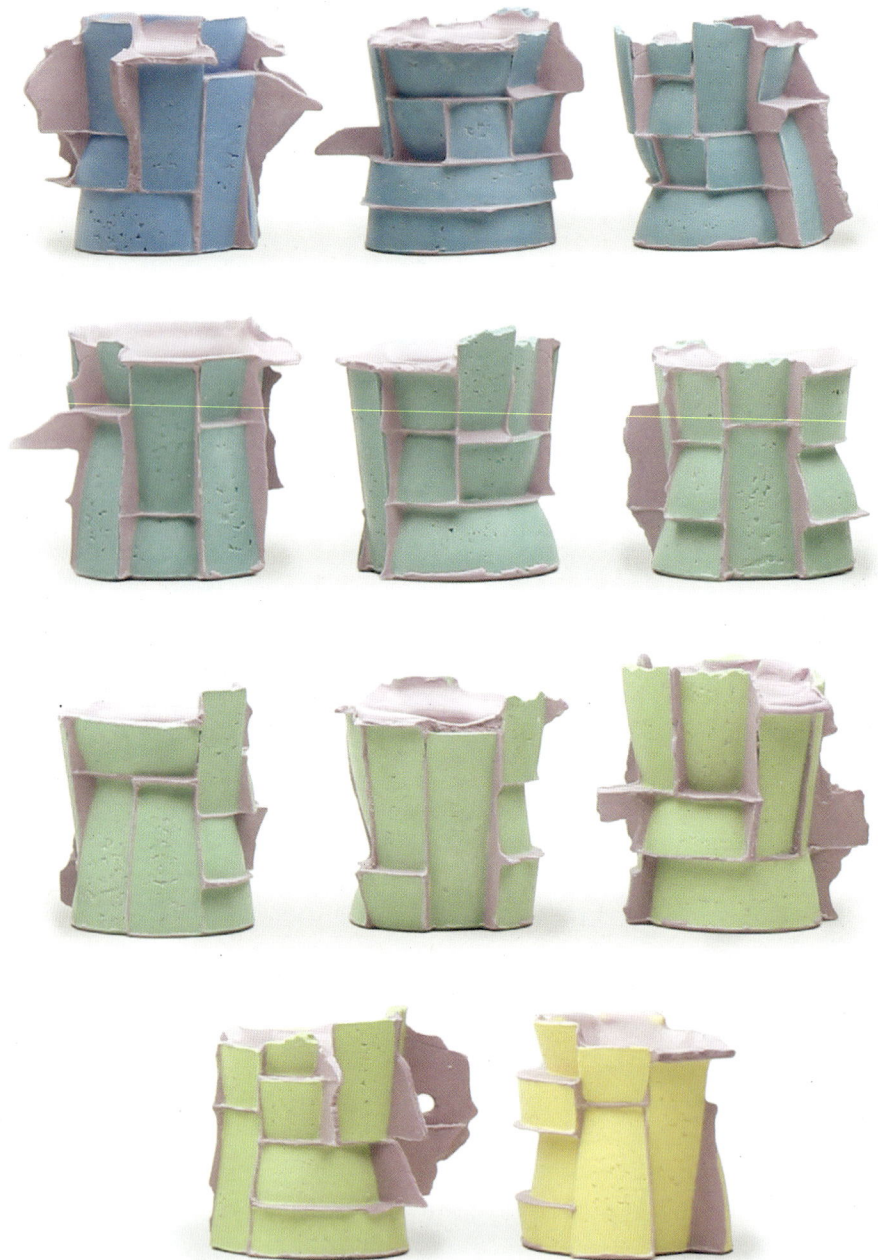

THE INFINITE ARCHITECTURE OF A VESSEL

KYLE JOHNS

"I try to push what perfection and precision mean into new places."

There is a sense of the infinite to Kyle Johns' architectural vessels. Every angle, every view and every exterior surface appears sectioned and resectioned. No matter where you look, like a Cubist painting rendered in the third dimension, Kyle's vessels present you with multiple chaotic viewpoints, and challenge the outer edges of craft and the notion of the handmade, slip-cast object.

Kyle grew up just outside of Chicago, Illinois, and like so many in clay took his first ceramics class on a whim. He studied in Illinois, Ohio and Hungary, and has worked at Arrowmont School for the Arts and Crafts, Red Lodge Clay Center, Archie Bray Foundation and Harvard. Needless to say, this has meant a lot of moving around for Kyle, and subsequently, he has not had a stable studio space. "The changing of studios causes me to adapt to each new situation," he says. "Because of my nomadic lifestyle, I haven't purchased anything too cumbersome, such as a slip casting bench or a kiln. I make do with what I have and what is available in the studio in which I'm currently working."

The vessel anchors Kyle's practice: "I work mostly with vessels, which enables me to take larger risks with either the process or concept of the work at any given time. The work pushes both function and methodology to an extreme. I'm interested in the space we share, the relationship to the body and the impact objects have on us." He gleans inspiration from architects and designers who create and employ innovative construction methods and solutions. Kyle then applies these observations to familiar functional ceramic forms like a cup. "Ceramic history contains

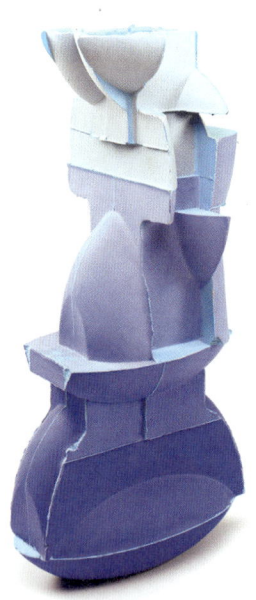

an immense amount of insight into how clay can be used, and with that it carries an enormous amount of tradition that is difficult to disregard," he says. "I search outside of the field of ceramics for cutting-edge ideas to keep me informed about current trends, and to bring a new perspective to my own practice."

By looking to architecture and design, his objects end up resembling futuristic buildings, but just like a building they also function as a vessel, whether it be a bowl, cup or vase. "My work is influenced by contemporary design, both of utilitarian ware and architecture," Kyle says. "For instance, architects choose to break up a living space, and the curves they use imply structure or movement—as well, the way a furniture designer decides on the shape and edges of a table. I look at what is happening with current design trends, contemplating their relevance in the ceramics field. The concepts and strategies employed by current designers broaden the scope of what can be possible with such an old material."

"We eat and drink from vessels, we drive and fly in vessels and we live in vessels. Vessels are relatable to everyone, no matter your class, gender or ethnicity. Vessels allow us to explore the modelling and segmentation of the fabrication and consumption in our world."

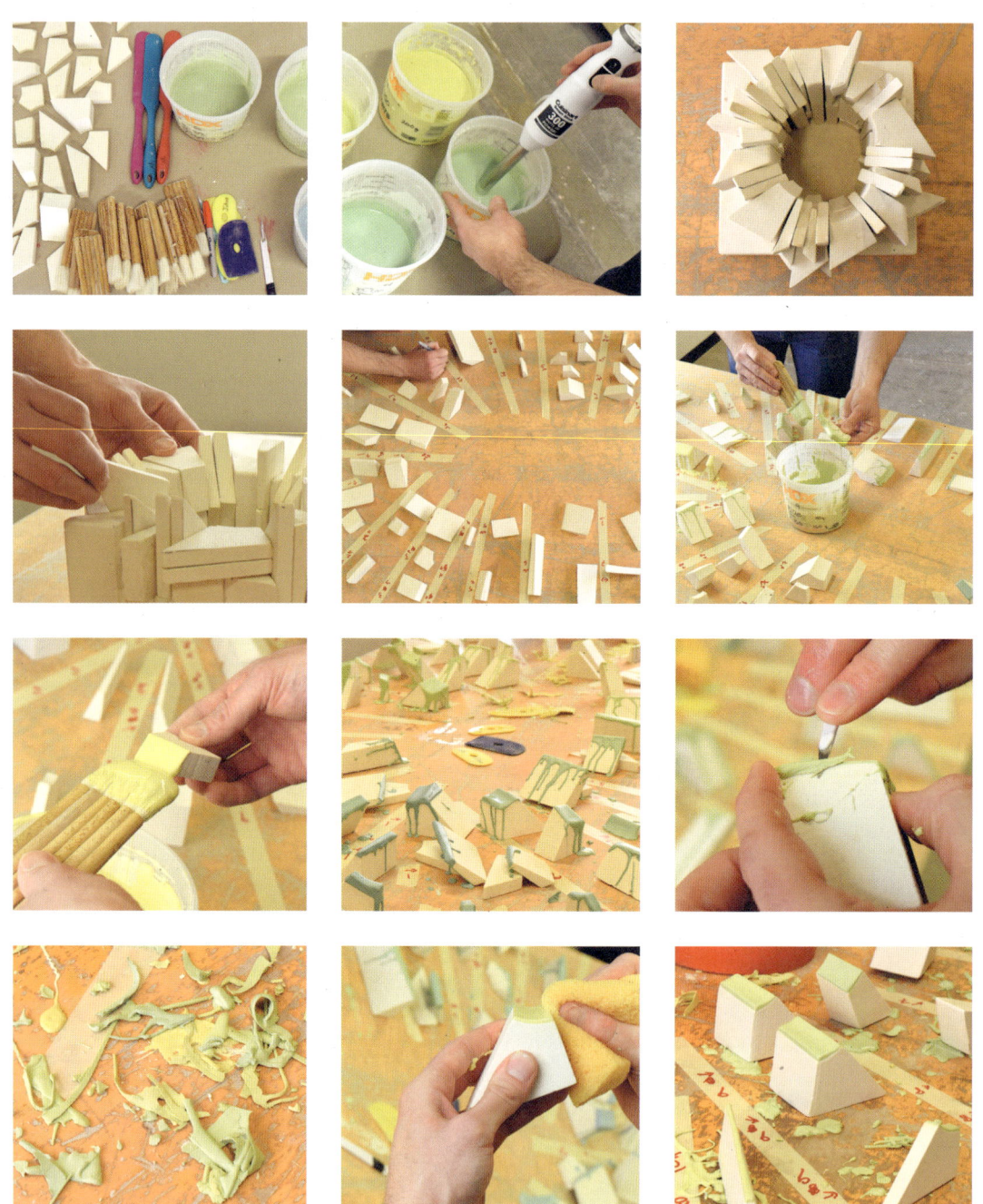

"Failure is what challenges my ideas and keeps me engaged. It involves varying degrees of risk, which I see as learning opportunities. I view failure at times as a motivator, which creates more questions and produces new ideas. I've worked with failure for so long that I look at it as another part of the process, a part in which I often revel."

KYLE JOHNS

Kyle aims to keep his day-to-day studio practice fresh and does so by embracing playful experimentation and exploration. "I feel like much of my life is chaotic, and the work's shifting components reflect that," he says. "I love to problem solve, so working with a method where the circumstances contain a degree of uncertainty fuels my interest." He purposefully balances time spent playfully experimenting with time making his known body of work. Play for Kyle includes experimenting with various application techniques for casting slip, creating and stacking mould parts or discovering what the negative interior and exterior spaces look like as positives. For Kyle, "Play is where the discoveries happen, whether it's a new glaze, colour blend, form or mould technique." ✻

kylejohnsceramics.com
@kylejohnsceramics

UNIVERSAL BUILDING BLOCKS

The plaster building block is at the core of Kyle's practice and is an indispensable tool. "I often play with mould parts, their positions, shapes and the colours applied onto them to generate new ideas," he explains. He first creates a primary mould form by arranging numerous plaster blocks together to form a negative vessel shape. Then, he paints coloured slip onto the building blocks with a bamboo wash brush designed to hold a substantial amount of slip. Once all the excess slip is removed using silicone ribs, knives and sponges, he reassembles the blocks, securing each in place with wads of clay so that when the void is filled with the liner slip, the mould will not burst apart. Pouring the liner slip requires a specific technique: "I pour into the centre of the mould, letting the slip raise up slowly, sealing all the mould parts together." Once the slip has had time to set, the excess casting slip is emptied out. The piece is demoulded at the leather-hard state and is fired with an electric kiln to ensure consistent and vibrant colours.

DEBORAH FISHER

JOY

WRITTEN BY CAROLE EPP

ELEVATED MOODS

SANDRA APPERLOO

Sandra Apperloo's beginnings in ceramics do not follow the commonly told story of art school or community centre pottery classes. Since 2013 she has been writing the ArtisticMoods blog, a curated collection of all genres of art and illustration that inspire her. Sharing the work of makers from around the world was a passion that, in turn, drove Sandra to become a successful maker in her own right. After years of writing about ceramics, it was her turn to get muddy. Sandra took courses at Noot & Swart Ceramics in Utrecht, Netherlands, and with the generous support of instructors Suus Notenboom and Ralph Swart, has remained captivated by the material ever since. Consequently, she now finds herself building her reputation under a new business name: The Pottery Parade. Sandra's days are now filled with mess and creation in the studio and less time blogging in front of a computer screen.

The Pottery Parade is a relatively young business, but Sandra has already cracked the code of how to make a living through her art practice. Nothing comes without growing pains, however, and Sandra has learned over time to prioritize organization in order to take on all the tasks associated with running a business. She takes care of all the administration, planning, social media and marketing, sales and customer service, save for a bit of help with shipping orders. Sandra humbly admits that she still has much to learn in the ceramics field; it really is an endless learning process. Thus, she dedicates time to exploring new things to expand her skills and broaden her audience.

"Usually, the items that I make have a functional character in some way. I mostly like to create plant pots, vases and dishes, and at times ornaments, too. I do feel my work is moving more towards becoming a sculpture—or let's say a functional sculpture—as I am becoming more and more fascinated by this as well."

BRINGING THE WORK TO LIFE

To mentally prepare for each workweek, and to set the stage for building new pots, Sandra begins with a clean studio. Her studio is located in her home in Utrecht. It is a quiet space with lots of light where she creates her character portraits on bowls, vases, cups, plates and planters. Many of Sandra's forms begin on the potter's wheel. This, she says, is one of her favourite stages of the process. She then sculpts the faces of her figurative characters, and then brings them to life by painting them. "I love painting the pieces, too, as it's when I get to express a lot of creativity and I can finally get to work on ideas I have had in my mind when sculpting a piece," she says. "Experimenting with new ideas is very important in my process. When I try a new design or pattern, I feel like I am waking up, and I am reminded of why I love creating ceramics so much. It has become a rule of mine to always include new things in my collections. This can be anything from a new pattern or design to a new type of item."

"I usually don't have an exact idea or design before starting off with a new piece. I first create the body of the piece on the pottery wheel or by hand. Once that is finished, I come up with a design and pattern that I feel complements its current shape. Working like this helps me to stay open to changes and new ideas when I am in the process of creating. It also prompts me to try out new designs when I feel it fits the pot or vase better. Although pieces don't always turn out as I expect or hope, working with an open mind has led to surprising results!" ✤

"What is most important for me at the moment is that I can build myself a future where I can continue to run The Pottery Parade with creative freedom. It's what makes this journey amazing. Within that freedom, I hope to explore many new ideas and techniques that will hopefully help me to continue to develop my artistic voice."

thepotteryparade.com
@thepotteryparade

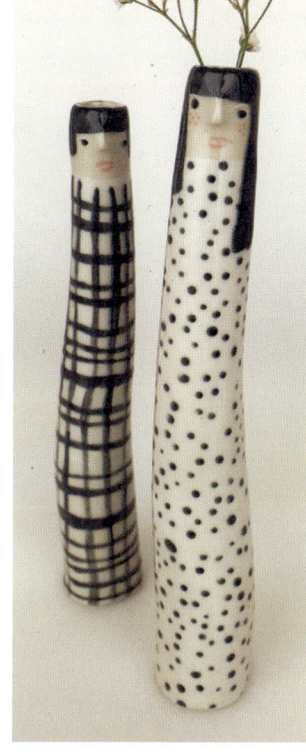

INSPIRATION

Because Sandra has made a name for herself blogging about the art that inspires her, one can virtually go down the rabbit hole of posts on ArtisticMoods to see the evolution of her tastes over the years. "I feel that the style of my work is drawn from a mix of inspiration from the contemporary artists and illustrators I wrote about on my blog for many years," she says. "Being inspired by imagery I love is what triggers me to sculpt, paint and try out new things. It has helped me to grow my own creative voice." These explorations, she says, are very important. "It keeps it all fun! It's an excellent reminder of what I love about creating ceramics."

"I love illustration, cuteness and soft-coloured, quirky things. I'd say I am a pretty cheerful person and I love to have a smile on my face. It may all sound a bit too cliché, but I honestly hope these are the things that are reflected in my work as well. I'd like to trigger my audience's imagination and put a smile on their face."

ILLUSTRATED NOSTALGIA

INGELA ARRHENIUS

Stockholm-based illustrator and designer Ingela Arrhenius has been working and building her international career since the early 1990s. With a background in advertising and graphic design, Ingela set up as a freelance illustrator and has had her work showcased internationally in advertising campaigns, magazine and book publications and editorial work.

Ingela's style is inspired by her love of bygone eras of design. While specific narratives or subjects in her illustrations change over time, this aesthetic leaning has remained her anchor point and brand for 30 years. Her work exists almost like a time capsule, a preservation of the past, that now in the context of contemporary media stands as a leader in the popular design trend of returning to vintage aesthetics. Her vintage-inspired typography and illustrations are geared towards children and collectors of childhood ephemera. In the most recent years of her career, Ingela's main focus has been illustrating children's books and toys, but sure enough, ceramics entered the picture as well.

Ingela has always described herself as a lover of objects. As a collector, flea market trips and antiquing adventures always began with a hunt for ceramic treasures. Ingela's rich understanding of object design is essentially self-taught, gained through her collection. She has yet to undertake studies in ceramics practice; instead, she relies on partnerships with industry to produce ceramic wares based on her designs. Ingela also purchases vintage ceramics at thrift stores and repurposes them by adding her own hand-painted illustrations.

"Always seek in yourself what you want to explore, what you miss doing, and move in that direction. Never stop finding new ways to express yourself."

Raising two children has meant living a life surrounded by the colours, textures and noise of childhood. This energy and vibrancy is a poignant part of Ingela's illustrative style. The play and busy energy of children is mirrored in her illustrations, which visually transform the ceramic vessel forms they inhabit. The ceramic forms she chooses to work with are functional as well as decorative, as she intends for her line of designed ceramic ware to be used as well as displayed as art in the home.

WORKING WITH INDUSTRY

Ingela's work process begins with "a feeling" of what she wants to present. Simple, rough pencil sketches come next, then she completes the bulk of the illustrations in a digital format. Working with industry partners in ceramics saves her from the many stresses and potential technical failures of the material: glaze faults, slumping forms or kiln misfires. But don't take that as implying that the work involved in illustrating her ceramics is easy. "It can happen that when I get pics of the first clay shapes from the factory I realize I might have failed in my illustrations and descriptions of how I want it to look," Ingela says. "So, of course, I am always worried when I get the final product. And I can see that, oh no, the mouth is too far from the nose, etc. But it's just me who sees that, no one else, if you understand what I mean." Problem solving on her hand-painted vintage dishes helps with the design process for her industry-partnered work. In hand painting wares, Ingela has the freedom to play, redo, remix and see immediately how form and illustration can integrate.

DIVERSIFYING PRODUCT LINES

All facets of Ingela's design business support her overall success and sustainability as an artist. As she says, "Looking at my business, ceramics is just a part of it. I do books and toys, etc., so I couldn't live off just my ceramic work." Ingela's brand is known for including textiles and fabrics, wallpaper for the home, and stationery. This broad range of items means her customers range from people purchasing affordable, mass-produced items, to those interested in one-of-a-kind pieces of art. What's next for Ingela? "Wood. I need to work more with wood." And she says she wants to take a ceramics course soon. It will be lovely to see how her work changes as she starts making her own ceramic forms. ❊

"For me, success is doing exactly what you want— you can live off your creativity, and it is loved by others. And you also have to have time to experiment so that you develop."

"Play is important. That is why painting on secondhand ceramics has been important—because there I can be totally free!"

STUDIO

During a typical day, Ingela takes care of the business side of things first off in the morning. Life/work balance is very important to her, so a portion of her day is set aside for time with friends and intensive triathlon training, both of which she is passionate about. In the afternoons and evenings, Ingela works alone in her studio, where she is surrounded by her vast collection of visual inspiration. Her children are grown, so her ability to maintain this life/work balance has greatly improved over the years.

ingelaparrhenius.com
@ingelaparrhenius

PATTERN, PROCESS AND PUNS

KAITLYN BRENNAN

Generally speaking, "ugly-cute" doesn't sound like a compliment to one's work, unless you are Ontario-based ceramic artist Kaitlyn Brennan, who thinks that it is a hilarious accolade. Kaitlyn is looking for a different type of compliment. Her aim as an artist is to make functional work that is not overly colour coordinated but rather contains bursts of colour and patterns mixed with pop culture references and puns.

"Ceramics have always been part of my life," says Kaitlyn. "I grew up in a farming family surrounded by objects that have been used for generations. These items were part of our everyday life, they had meaning and value to us, and they connected our fields and labouring directly to our table."

There is something energetic in the surfaces of Kaitlyn's work and how they envelop the forms she creates. They are bold and colourful statements that bring not only the element of fun to the dinner table but also "a multisensory experience involving aesthetics, form and ergonomics." The layered depth of Kaitlyn's work is drawn from her earlier soda-fired student work when she studied at the University of Florida and the Alberta University of the Arts. This intense type of firing requires a specific kiln that is difficult to access and expensive to own. After art school, Kaitlyn switched techniques and began working with red earthenware clay layered with slip to obtain a multi-layered surface styling that is now unique to her pots.

"I want my pots to be a highlight of someone's morning, something that can make them smile even on the darkest winter day. Knowing what subjects are making people happy is part of my research. After that, I can figure out all the fun ways to work with that theme."

"The value of the handmade is derived from more than simply a remnant left from the potter's hand. It is about the potter's careful consideration and attentiveness to each ware individually—from throwing each cup to pulling and attaching each handle, to trimming each plate."

WORK OUTSIDE THE STUDIO

Kaitlyn currently makes work out of her home studio in Ottawa. It is a basement studio that she has filled to the brim with work and equipment, forcing her studio dog, Stout, to sleep next door in the laundry room. Kaitlyn's home studio is a workable space that allows her to juggle work with raising two young children with her wife. Ceramic processes often require as much attention and monitoring as kids, and the ability to check on the drying stages of pots or to pop in to work for a few minutes throughout the day is invaluable. "I usually get in a few evenings a week after the boys are in bed, a weekend day, and maybe if we get rained out at work an actual weekday workday," she says. "It is constantly changing as my family grows."

Kaitlyn works part time as a stonemason. "I enjoy being a mason," says Kaitlyn. "It is challenging, hands-on and involves constant problem solving, with opportunities to develop my skills and try to do the best masonry work possible, just like I try to make the best

pots possible." Having outside work relieves financial pressure so that she does not need to be entirely dependent on art sales. Without that pressure, she feels she can make better, more considered work in the studio. "I have felt guilty, that I should want to make pots full time, and that I must not be that serious of an artist if I don't. I have struggled to get over that guilt, to realize it doesn't matter if someone makes pots full time or not. For me, it matters if the work is good and I am constantly trying to improve."

Kaitlyn stays creatively motivated by exploring ways of making work that doesn't feel like work. Each piece is unique, which removes the boredom of repetition and allows each studio session to feel like play. Kaitlyn has been successful in building relationships with wholesale clients that honour her one-of-a-kind work and respect her need to constantly evolve and challenge herself. ✽

"My pots have multiple layers of texture and imagery that create depth, and hopefully an atmospheric quality. They are bright and colourful, and covered with layers of fun designs. The designs and themes I choose are things I like and are fun to draw—like flowers, pizza and pineapples— or things that I think are funny to put on my pottery that maybe aren't obviously funny. For example, I'm a lesbian artist who makes mugs with beavers and tacos on them."

"There is so much I really like about clay, but I always come back to the same thought—practice and dedication matter. I don't think you can fake your way to a good pot; you've got to put in the hours and the effort, and be self-critical and able to constantly push yourself to make a better pot than the one before."

kaitlynbrennan.com
@kaitlynabrennan

PROCESS

"My pots are very time intensive," Kaitlyn says. "I have thought about simplifying my process so I can make more work faster, but that wouldn't be the work I want to make. I am more likely to add more steps to each piece than simplify them."

At first glance, it is the bold colours of Kaitlyn's underglazes and sgraffito drawings that are most noticeable in her work. Sgraffito is a historical technique of scratching through one surface to unveil a contrasting surface beneath, used for centuries by craftspeople. Take a closer look and there are also layers of texture, etchings hidden under a white slip, and elements that are pushed out of the surface to make the form of the vessel more tactile.

"I use a red clay body that I texture with tools, including a faux wood grain paint tool, an old spool, a dog toy and Kinder Surprise toys," she explains. "I puff clay out through stencils I've made that correspond with the theme I'm using. Before I finally get to applying slip I draw designs into the clay using a pointed wooden tool. I mix my white slip thin so it doesn't evenly or fully cover the red clay when I dip my pots. If after I dipped the slip looks a bit too even, I will lightly mist with water to get the slip moving. The layers of texture show through the slip, creating a really fun canvas to draw designs into. After that, it's just sgraffito, bisque, underglaze and glaze."

CREATIVE COMPANIONS

DEBORAH FISHER

Deborah Fisher's upbringing in a creative and collaborative family environment is enough to make anyone envious. "When I was growing up, we had a big round table in the family room that we could do projects on," she says. "My mother taught me to sew, and I made a lot of dolls and animals. I was using polymer clay when it only came in white and you had to paint it. We had all of those wonderful open-ended materials like pom-poms and fabric and paper." The passing down of generational knowledge and the fostering of creativity is a beautiful thing, and her own daughters now enjoy a similar upbringing. Her father imparted to her his knowledge of clay—they still share a kiln today.

Deborah's first passion, fibre arts, led her to academic studies. Ceramics, though ever-present, always seemed to be on the sidelines. However, a residency at the internationally respected John Michael Kohler Art Center and the time spent taking ceramics classes with her father at a local art league eventually made Deborah want to combine ceramics with her already established quilting and textile arts practice. She still calls herself an "accidental ceramicist" who would rather not be categorized. "I approach any material thinking about what it can do and how it can fit into what I want to make," she explains. "As an object maker, clay is just one of the many materials that I use."

Deborah's world is full of life, colour, pattern and story—and the ceramic worlds she creates through her clay characters are, too. Her figures are imbued with life, whimsy and inspiring energy. Since childhood, Deborah has been creating characters of one sort or another—dolls, animals, hybrid creatures—each with a cacophony of materials, textures and patterns.

"My work tends to speak to other makers. They appreciate that the utilitarian can be fun. They embrace the quirky, the imaginary and the weird."

MISCELLANY FOR MAKERS

For Deborah, "ceramic work is a collection of charming miscellany for makers." She has a fondness for graphic and pattern design, colour combinations and the small, subtle things in life. Deborah's business, Fish Museum + Circus, is composed of objects that brighten the workspaces of other makers. "I make pincushions and thread holders for sewists, buttons, brush rests for painters, and objects that celebrate the maker's hand, the creative eye and other essential tools of making. I love the utility and the fun that objects can bring to the work. I love that what I make can not only be a part of someone's life, but also part of their creative practice."

"The characters I create have evolved into a menagerie of 'thingimals,'" describes Deborah. "They may resemble an actual animal. Kind of. With a horn, or a beak. Or not: a funny nose or an odd appendage. They are all unique, with whimsical personalities. They are sidekicks for the studio, sewing room and worktable. Human faces and figures also appear in the collection. Their simple faces of dots for eyes and a line for a mouth create a serene muse for the maker. I create colour, pattern and texture using bright underglaze and techniques such as sgraffito, and cut paper stencils, as well as with a variety of materials such as wool for the pincushions and ribbon for tails. The work is a way for me to express the characters in my story. My objects live between my actual world and an imaginary world."

It's no surprise that play is an important part of Deborah's process. Characters reveal themselves to her through the making process; she may start with a specific idea and get led away on an adventure. Responding to the moment is an essential nature of play. "It becomes like a puzzle to solve," she explains. ✼

DEBORAH FISHER

"I get really lovely messages from people who follow me on social media, or who get my email newsletter. Whenever I am not sure of what I am doing, I remember that. And I try to remind myself that making is a journey and an adventure. It is the heart and soul of who I am."

"Clay and I have an uncertain relationship. We are working hard to get to know each other better, and while I think we will eventually come to an understanding, things are still a bit tenuous. My process is influenced by my textile sensibility. The use of underglaze to create more graphic colour and pattern is what comes naturally."

SURFACE DECORATION

While for some ceramic artists the technical, chemistry side of the process can be inspirational, this is not the case for Deborah. "I prefer minimal equipment and tools, and staunchly avoid things like glaze chemistry," she says. "I love to see what other artists do with wonderful glazes, glaze chemistry and technique, but it is not in my nature to embrace that in my own work." For her, she explains, "the beauty of handmade *is* the maker's hand. The directness of the hand on the clay is what draws me to the process."

For surface decoration, Deborah uses techniques such as underglaze painting, cut paper stencils and sgraffito—underglaze, of course, being one of the most immediate ways to bring vibrant colours to clay surfaces. "My process is influenced by my textile sensibility," she says. "The use of underglaze to create more graphic colour and pattern is what comes naturally." Textiles and quilting continue to make up a part of her practice alongside the clay; they are just as quirky and as full of life, from Claes Oldenburg–inspired giant ice cream cone pillows to published books and tutorials on quilting and sewing projects. Deborah approaches her practice in mixed-media terms: "Fibre, textiles, pattern design, graphic design, printmaking. Sgraffito and block printing are so related. I find sgraffito to be a very interesting process. I like the directness of the mark-making, the taking away of material in a way that can be both drawing and sculpture."

Deborah also uses cut paper stencils to block out areas of colour on her forms. Paper stencils aren't reusable, so thankfully her local library has a Library of Things. "They have a Cricut machine that you can check out. It has been a great tool for me to be able to make multiple and more complicated paper cuts. I can only use each paper cut once so this has been a game-changer for what I can do."

fishmuseumandcircus.com
@fishmuseum

BOLD AND CONTROLLED

ADRIENNE ELIADES

"Ceramics is one of the most ancient industries, dating back thousands of years. The idea that I will be able to create something truly unique is unreasonable. However, I love the challenge of offering a fresh take on a classic."

Not many people can say that they've circumnavigated the globe, but in college, Adrienne Eliades did a semester at sea. "It was a life-changing experience," she says. Perhaps out of rebellion from 18 years spent with her family in a high-rise condominium, since her late teenage years, Adrienne has been on the move, travelling to five out of seven continents. Now she is settling down in Vancouver, Washington, in the beautiful Pacific Northwest.

The vibrant arts community in the Vancouver/Portland area is taming Adrienne's desire to travel, and she might lay down roots for the first time in years. She currently maintains a full-time career as an artist, educator and studio coordinator at the Idyllwild Arts summer program. Adrienne enjoys the energy that these different opportunities bring: teaching is a passion, and jobs that provide a change of pace from the studio always feed back into her artistic work as inspiration. "I absolutely love being involved in a craft school," she says. "It's a dream job for me. These types of alternatives to academic experiences can have such a huge impact on students of all ages. I love being a part of that and getting to live at an adult art camp for a month out of the year. The energy there is so vibrant—a welcome change of pace from solo studio life."

Adrienne sells her work through several galleries and retail shops, and feels she is at a stage in her career wherein most opportunities are worth exploring. Since studying at grad school in Florida, Adrienne has sought out grants, awards, exhibitions and publications in order to establish her career. On top of that, she has been steadily building an online presence to

get her work directly to her audience. "I feel that people want to buy experiences more than objects today. When buying an object, it helps if the buyer has a direct line to me. They can meet me, talk to me in person or on social media, ask me questions and make a personal connection. They feel that they are not only buying an object but a piece of me and my practice."

A FRESH TAKE ON TRADITION

Adrienne makes design-focused tableware that exudes a nostalgic 1980s palette and geometric style; it's a fresh take on familiar but vintage trends. "When I design work I always look back, back to design movements, to historical and contemporary pottery from different cultures, and to iconic forms that define generations of domestic use," describes Adrienne. Her work is highly refined and technical but still full of life and play. Her love of "order, control, organization and cleanliness" is immediately apparent, and she plays with that visual language to evoke emotional responses connected to memory. "My energetic designs are communications with the user, revealing their unique interpretations as the subconscious mind attempts to make sense of the visual stimuli."

THE ILLUSIONIST

The clean, refined lines of Adrienne's functional forms trick most people into thinking that she slip-casts all her wares. In reality, she combines wheel-thrown, hand-built and slip-cast components throughout her work. Her mugs are complex: they tend to have all of these construction methods mixed up in their assemblage. "I am not interested in expressing the inherent materiality of clay but rather using its malleability to create streamlined forms with clean lines and gentle organic curves punctuated by asymmetry," Adrienne

says. She likes to play with the viewer, forcing them to question and investigate the construction of her work.

"I am a perfectionist," Adrienne admits, and one can see the attention to detail in the quality of her wares. She has a hard time accepting anything less than her high expectations, and this resilience was put to the test in grad school. "I failed my second-year review," she recalls. "This was beyond heartbreaking for me. I worked so hard and I couldn't wrap my head around how effort, intention and hard work wasn't enough. Later, I understood that what I was making and how I was talking about it just did not match up. Now I am grateful for that experience because it was an awakening. It ultimately made my work better and will forever be a reminder that failure does not define who you are; how you deal with it does. Now when I have a perceived failure I use that experience, those hurt emotions, to make better work, remembering that some things need to fail in order to put my work in a truly vulnerable state. After all, vulnerability is where the magic happens."✻

"Functional objects don't have to be basic. I love the challenge of making objects that look as good as they work and feel."

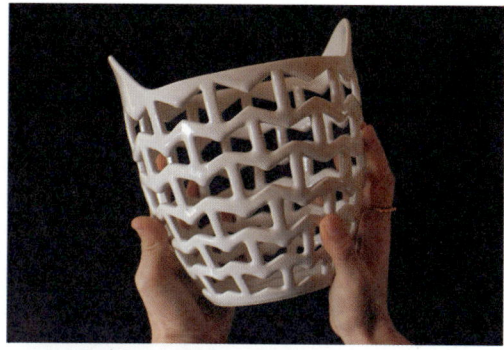

adrienneeliades.com
@bugaboo_eyes

DESIGNING FORMS

Adrienne's father is a chef and restaurateur, and her mother works with him, so for Adrienne there is a natural progression of thought from cooking to serving. She quite literally grew up in restaurant kitchens, amidst the bustle and noise, and the smells and tastes. "Because of this upbringing and my Greek heritage, I have always been inspired by food and how it can bring people together," she says. "I am focused on creating handmade objects that encourage connection between one another and the food we eat."

"I design new forms based on food specificity," Adrienne explains. Considering proportion and utility, she does historical research while looking at contemporary objects. "I do this for two reasons: first, to see what's been done, and second, to be able to design with a keen sense of departure to somehow make that form my own. I then sketch different solutions to that form." Selecting from her best sketches, Adrienne prototypes them nearly to scale—including ideas of decoration. "In this way," she says, "I can get an idea of how form, function and surface will harmonize in space. Usually, I stray from my sketch and give myself permission to play and depart from my original idea. Thinking through doing allows for new solutions that I could not theorize by simply putting pen to paper. As I go along, I make Tyvek templates for the pieces so I can replicate them easily." She makes notes of clay weight, dimensions and order of construction, relying on these notes to make consistent work.

HUMOUR IN CERAMICS

RICHARD NICKEL

Richard Nickel is a multidisciplinary artist based out of Norfolk, Virginia. He is well known for his ceramics, but is equally as respected for his illustrations, animations, murals and public art projects. For Richard, a fairly cohesive aesthetic comes out of the ebb and flow among these different mediums, each expanding upon and inspiring the others. Richard also runs a ceramic growler business called Norfolk Growler Company. To say that his plate is full is an understatement. He is an artist who craves living in the moment and appreciates the temporal nature of life, so he feels an urgency to make art while he has the time.

Richard's work is all about humour and the human condition. "I find humour to be one of the most subversive art forms available to humans for expression," he says. "Humour disarms prejudice, it disarms angry people, it opens a door for transformation into thought in ways that other artwork cannot." There is a long history of using humour in ceramics. Richard finds inspiration from the art of ancient Indigenous Mimbres potters, Carolina "face jugs" and folk art, or what has been labelled outsider art. "Although the art's original intent may or may not have been humour, a contemporary perspective can often find comedic value. These artists looked at the world of contemporary art from the sidelines, never being fully accepted. They built a reputation on thumbing their noses at 'the system' and created artwork that often used absurdity to get the point across. It is only now that these outsiders have become pillars of our art schools."

Richard makes his cartoonish characters to express aspects of the human condition. He wants them to exist as representations of joyfulness and fun. But

"Art is often seen as an introverted, solitary experience involving serious thought and messages. Frequently overlooked are examples of the lighter side of human existence—comedy. Art, like life, is a balance between comedy and tragedy. Shakespeare's darkest plays were balanced with keen wit and humour. My intent in much of my artwork is to reveal the purpose of humour in art and to show that, in art, comedy and tragedy are dependent on each other for a deeper understanding of the human condition."

"When I create my ceramic sculptures, I pay particular attention to the outline of the form. They are simple and complex at the same time, and, to the best of my ability, mirror the drawings I've done to create the feelings the lines give me. I single fire everything. I hate labouring over work, as it loses its freshness."

he also aims to stop you in your tracks, make you pause in the moment and make you consider the nature of things around you. "It's not all about humour as much as the balance between comedy and tragedy," he explains. "I feel this must be apparent. Just like how life cannot be without comedy and tragedy, or happiness and sadness, art should also reflect the same balance." Richard sees these characters as recordings of this particular moment in our culture. "Humour is difficult," he says.

GARDEN INSPIRED

The bright colours and quirky characters of his work are drawn from his fascination for life and the natural world. "I look to tomatoes, stems and grapes, and all these beautiful forms found in nature are always so much more interesting than any artwork I've seen. I'm often astounded at what the earth can grow and what can be found in nature. I'm often astounded at the human ability to destroy the very thing that gives us life."

"Humour is subversive. Poetry is veiled truth. Life is bittersweet and people who laugh the loudest often cry the most. I want my art to speak to these people who feel so deeply about nature, they listen to the sounds of songbirds and they look for the drift of clouds over the treetops."

STUDIO AND PROCESS

Richard's design and ceramic work is a solo endeavour, done out of two studios, one at his home and the other at Norfolk Growler Company. The mural works, however, involve a team of artists to see the projects completed. During a typical studio workweek, Richard may create up to three sculptures at once. The back-and-forth on the pieces means that each piece can be set up and dried as needed and not get overworked, and time in between stages isn't wasted. Richard creates his large pieces using a simple slab construction method. The work is decorated in the wet stage, with colours and glazes all at once, and then fired to temperature. This simplified process means he can cut down on production time and firing costs. ✻

"As an artist, I want to make a cosmic connection to the soul of a human."

INSPIRATION

Most of Richard's artistic influences come out of painting and drawing. "I've always been drawn to artists who express a deep love for family or humour or everyday existence. I appreciate people who, trained or untrained, appreciate life, and stop and look around them, whether it's at a field of trees in the distance or a window filled with light, and then document their experiences. These are the artists who remind us that life is fleeting and we need to stop take a breath and look at what's around us."

richardjnickel.weebly.com
@richardnickel

ACKNOWLEDGEMENTS

CAROLE EPP

For me, ceramics has always been about community. Back in my undergrad it was as much about learning how to fire kilns and mix glazes as it was organizing Friday night movie parties in the studio so we would all stay late and learn how to throw pots and eat pizza. Ceramic studios have always held some of my most cherished memories, as they also hold some of my dearest friends. Ceramics hooks people, it draws them in, steals them away from other creative disciplines and feeds the creative soul like no other material.

Building a life and career in ceramics has opened me up to so many incredible opportunities that I would have never imagined. Much of what I hope to achieve in my career in clay is to earn a place in this community through supporting it through whatever means I can. This book for me is a continuation of work I've been doing to bring attention to the clay community over the last 14 years through my blog, Musing About Mud, and the collective Make and Do Ceramics. This publication is a space to celebrate and elevate makers in our community. Here we share artists' stories, what inspires them, and we provide a space to pause and really look at the artwork each artist creates. This publication is a record of just some of the astonishing artists the ceramics community has to offer. I hope the pages herein will inspire you, challenge your definition of the possibilities of ceramics and lead you to search out other artists around the globe that make powerful work with the most humblest of materials: the ground beneath our feet. From where I stand, ceramics is a community full of ideas, innovation, passion and unique processes. I want to shout from the mountaintops about this generous and talented community of makers. I'm grateful for the place that this community has offered me at their table.

I'm thankful to Janine Vangool for this unique opportunity to contribute to the documentation of the ceramics field at this particular time in history. I've long been in absolute awe of her publications and know that they have contributed greatly to inspiring my own creative path. Julia Krueger is a writer I've been trying to work with for years and I'd like to express what an honour it is to share these pages with her. Thanks as well to Correy Baldwin for your keen eye and catching all the grammatical hiccups and making me sound better!

To my family, Jord, Elliott, Jasper and my sister Michelle—you all rock and I hope you know why! I'm forever grateful, for without your support I could never follow the dreams and demands of my passionate heart. ✻

ACKNOWLEDGEMENTS

JULIA KRUEGER

Some of my earliest memories involve ceramics and books, and no, they don't involve precious pots tumbling off bookshelves but are memories of my siblings and I being allowed to roam and explore a specific used bookstore in Regina, Saskatchewan, where an amazing ceramics collection was on display, nestled in amongst stories from other worlds and other times. When I first left Saskatchewan for university in the mid-1990s, I found myself sitting through hours of undergraduate art history classes but only ever really seeing Greek vases! Where were all those magical contemporary examples I had seen as a child? At that point in time, I took it upon myself to learn as much as I could about the material and its history, and in the process, over the course of my career, I have met so many incredible people from the craft and ceramics communities who have enriched my life in countless ways. Ceramics is about more than just clay or Greek pots; it is about community, problem solving, ingenuity, beauty, function, creativity, criticality and wonder. It is a conduit to other worlds, possibilities and modes of thinking. I feel so lucky to be a part of the ceramics community and to be trusted with telling some of its stories.

With a project such as this there are so many people to thank, as I cannot ever begin the task of writing alone. I would first and foremost like to thank Janine Vangool for believing in me, for supporting and encouraging me through my painfully slow writing pace and for giving me the opportunity to work on such a unique project. With her expert project management skills and business sense, she has skillfully kept me on track, and I have learned so much from her about how to lead a large project such as this. In addition, it is an honour to be a part of one of her beautiful publications, as Janine's contribution to the discourse of Canadian craft and design is enormous. It has also been such a joy to work with Carole Epp, a ceramist who I deeply admire and respect. Her work is amazing and her community involvement and unyielding drive and bravery is inspirational, and she pushes me to consider things I have never considered before. I am so lucky to have had the opportunity to work with both of these women, and I hope to do so again. I also must acknowledge all the artists who took the time to submit such amazing images and thoughtful answers to our questions: thank you for your trust, words, work and participation. Thank you also to Correy Baldwin for his editing expertise. And finally, I must thank my family and especially my sister, Yolande, who are always there to support and push me forward. Without them I wouldn't be able to explore all that ceramics has to offer. ✻

AUTHOR BIOGRAPHIES

CAROLE EPP

Carole Epp is a ceramic artist, curator, researcher and writer based out of Saskatoon, Saskatchewan. Known internationally through exhibitions of her work, she has also contributed to the critical writing of craft through numerous publications. Respected as a curator, she has been involved with curating and organizing a number of ceramic and craft-based exhibitions. She has travelled extensively to teach workshops and to engage with communities of craft practice internationally. In 2017 she received the Artist of the Year award from *Ceramics Monthly* in recognition of her years of advocating for the ceramic community through such projects as Musing About Mud and Make and Do Ceramics.

caroleepp.com
@musingaboutmud

JULIA KRUEGER

Julia Krueger maintains an active writing, curatorial and research practice grounded in material culture and craft theory. Over the course of her academic career, she has studied art history (BA), ceramics (BFA), Canadian art history (MA) and visual culture (PhD). Julia has taught at the University of Western Ontario, Luther College, University of Regina and Alberta University of the Arts, and is currently the registrar for the permanent collection at SK Arts. Her writing has been published in various exhibition catalogues and in the *Encyclopedia of Saskatchewan* and *Studio Magazine*. She has co-curated the exhibitions *Hansen-Ross Pottery: Pioneering Fine Craft on the Canadian Prairies*, *Tactile Desires: The Work of Jack Sures* and *Victor Cicansky: The Gardener's Universe*.

@yoyolli